Originally published in Germany under the title
"Korea – Meine kulinarische Reise ins Land der vielen Wunder"
by Christian Verlag, in 2019.

Published in the United States in 2023 by Culina Cookbooks, an imprint of

Clevo Books
530 Euclid Ave #45
Cleveland, Oh 44115
www.clevobooks.com

©2019 Christian Verlag

English translation copyright ©2023 Clevo Books

Library of Congress Control Number: 2022947456
ISBN: 978-0-9973052-4-1
eBook ISBN: 978-1-68577-003-7

Printed in the USA

Translator: Jill Sommer
Editor: Michelle Standley
English language typesetting: Ron Kretsch

First American Edition

SARAH HENKE

KOREA

My Culinary Homecoming

With 60 Authentic Recipes

Photographs: Jan C. Brettschneider

CULINA

CONTENTS

My trip to the land of many wonders

I am not a tour guide who explores every detail. I set out to experience the land in which I was born for myself. In other words, I'm sharing my very personal trip to Korea with you. The fact that this trip focuses on food and meals and the way the people in Korea treat them is also something personal. Because I'm a chef, this is a big part of my life.

My travel destination is Korea, a country I left 34 years ago. Unfortunately, I know very little about my origins. I wasn't even two years old when someone found me wandering the streets of Seoul, in a part of the city that even back then was already pretty lively. I was probably born on February 23, 1982. My name was Young Sun Kim, which means "glorious and good natured." I could walk. I could say "NooNa." That's about all that I know.

People have often asked me why I haven't traveled to Korea before or whether I was curious to find out more about it or about my past. But I've always responded with a question: Do I really need to know more? After all, what matters most is who I am today and what I've made of my life since then. My parents have always been there, standing behind me. That's a lot more important than knowing more about my origins. And I have to admit, frankly, I've always been a little afraid to know more. I've feared finding out exactly where I came from, and worried about how that knowledge might impact me, maybe more than I would want it to. It's the sort of thing that you can't simply forget or pretend that you don't know once you do; afterwards you can't continue to live like you did before. That would most likely be the case here. There's probably some story behind why I was an orphan in the first place. Besides, I'm really happy with my family and my life today. In the end, that's what counts most.

In Lower Saxony, in the village where I grew up, there was a Korean woman who was married to a German. When I was still pretty young, my parents asked me whether I'd like to make her acquaintance and suggested that maybe she could also teach me Korean. But I didn't want to; I didn't feel like I needed it. I was German and had my parents. Why should I learn Korean, and do something that wasn't in any way related to my world?

At my restaurant, Yoso, a Michelin-starred, Asian restaurant located in a small town on the Rhine, I had sometimes experimented with Korean-inspired dishes. But I did not have any plans to test their authenticity with a visit to the country. Then a few years ago, Sonya Mayer, someone I knew who worked at the German publisher, Christian Verlag, put the idea in my head. Why not visit Korea accompanied by a photographer who would document my trip and then write a book about it? It would be part travelogue and part cookbook. Then everything happened fast: within less than a year they had booked me a trip with a travel agency that specializes in culinary tours. I barely had time to wrap my head around it: I was finally taking the trip that I had long imagined but had also somehow feared: I was returning to Korea.

The very last photo opportunity before leaving Germany.

TODAY is the big day that I've been anxiously awaiting. Today I'm flying to Korea. I'm still in disbelief. Less than 24 hours and I'll be in Seoul!

The itinerary and schedule arranged by the travel agency arrived a few days ago. Filled with anticipation, I started searching the Internet to find out where the different places were that we'd be visiting. On the agenda were stops in five cities in South Korea: Busan, Gyeongju, Andong, Seoul, Jeonju, and a temple in Baekyangsa. I'd be going to street markets and touring temples, one of which I'd be staying at overnight; taking a cooking class with a monk, Jeong Kwan (at that point I didn't know how famous this cooking class is; we'll get to that later); and visiting traditional Hanok villages. Would I get the chance to wear a Hanbok, the traditional Korean garment for women? A guide would also be showing me around the capital city, Seoul. What would Koreans be like? Apart from the days in which I'd be accompanied by a tour guide, I'd also have time to go out alone and make my own discoveries.

Much of the trip would revolve around food. The classic dishes such as bibimbap, kimchi, bulgogi are already on the schedule, and we'd be visiting a restaurant that serves fugu (puffer fish). Oh! I'm curious: Is the fugu that you can only get in Japan in select restaurants and prepared by fugu master chefs? Because if it's not, it can kill you!

It will definitely be a special trip. I'm curious about how I will feel there? So many things will be new to me. Up to now, everything I've known about Korea has come from two travel guidebooks that I read to learn a little more about the people, the culture, and the country that I come from.

I'll be taking the train to Frankfurt Airport. The train travels along the Rhine River — a beautiful region that I've really seen far too little of... I wonder if they also make wine in Korea? I pull up Facebook again. There are a lot of kind comments. My friends are happy for me that I'm taking this trip. "Good luck," "Take lots of pictures," "A journey back to your roots!" "Have a good flight." It's nice to know that so many people are part of it and wish me all the best.

Eckhardt / Young Sun Sarah

FROM ✈ TO
FRA ICN
Terminal 1   Terminal 1
Frankfurt Intl   Seoul Incheon International

LANDING
11:50
06Apr2018

BOARDING TIME   GATE
7:50   Check monitors

EUROPÄISCHE UNION
BUNDESREPUBLIK
DEUTSCHLAND

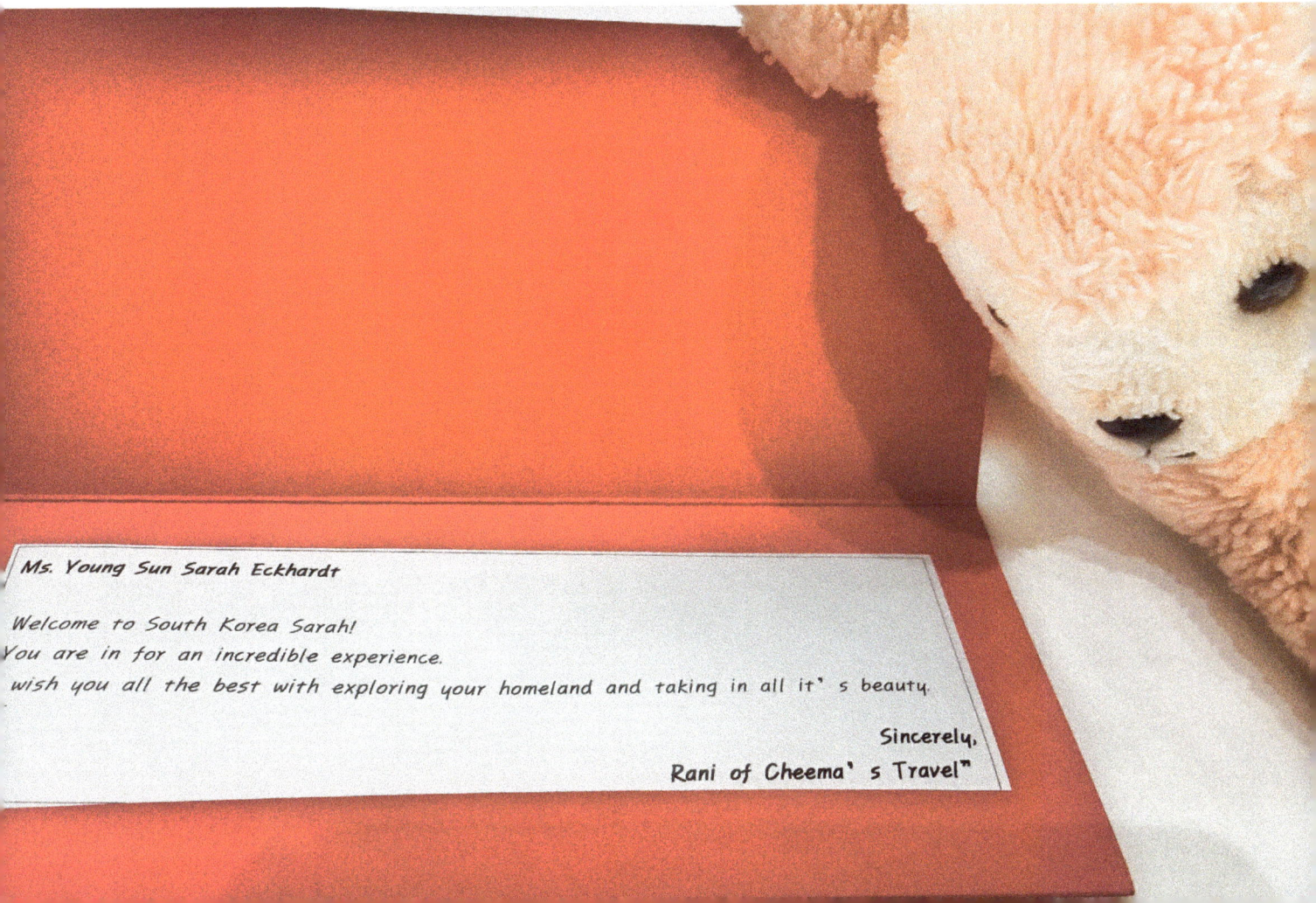

Ms. Young Sun Sarah Eckhardt

Welcome to South Korea Sarah!
You are in for an incredible experience.
I wish you all the best with exploring your homeland and taking in all it's beauty.

Sincerely,
Rani of Cheema's Travel™

BUSAN

Vibrant city by the sea

Day 1, April 6th. We land at the very modern Incheon Airport in Seoul. I'm exhausted from the long journey. Over ten hours on the airplane! We left Cologne at 5:15 p.m., and they are seven hours ahead here. Korea has seasons that are similar to those in Germany. So right now, in April, it's rather cool.

One of the first things I notice is that Koreans don't see me as a Western tourist. That makes me feel good somehow.

Half of all Korea's inhabitants live in Seoul — 25 million people. I'm in awe of that number when I make one of my first observations: for such a large city, everything runs incredibly smoothly. I think back on Bangkok. It has about 8 to 9 million inhabitants, and everything is extremely hectic and loud. Even our continued journey to Busan, the large port city in southeast Korea (with around 3.5 million inhabitants), comes off without a hitch. The ticket I purchased at the ticket vending machine has a seat reservation printed on it. There's no fare dodging in Korea. That's because a problem would emerge right away. You wouldn't have an assigned seat. That's probably why I wasn't checked by a conductor once during my three train trips in the country, the way that I might have been during such a trip in Germany. It's also very orderly on the platforms. You're only allowed to go onto the platform where your train is just before it departs. I didn't quite understand the reason for this. Nobody is hanging around on the platform; you have to wait in front of the train station. The rail network in Korea is really modern and organized. That's one of the many advantages of being a geographically small country. That's true for the mail too, which can often be delivered within a day. It's one of the reasons that online shopping is so popular here. I read that bit in my travel guide...but I am getting off track.

First destination: Busan The train trip takes another two and a half hours, and then I'm in Busan. To be honest, I don't remember much of the trip, because I'm pretty tired. I take a taxi to the hotel. Thanks to the tour guide, who emailed me an app in advance, I have all the information I need on my phone, and the addresses are also shown in Korean script so that I can get to the hotel safely. Despite being tired, I can't wait to try my first Korean meal tonight; my culinary tour finally starts. I know a little bit already about Korean cuisine. I know, for instance, that they serve the ingredients for the dishes separately so that the guest can create their own combinations themselves.

In 2014, I participated as a guest chef at the art and culture festival "Korea Live" in Dresden. I was really excited to get feedback from a Korean chef and restaurant owner about how Korean my dishes actually tasted. His verdict: "The dishes aren't very authentic, but the way you cook could make a lot of money in Korea." At the time, I didn't understand what he meant. Let's see if by the end of this trip I do!

Going out to eat for the first time. My first search for food begins. The hotel is very centrally located, so I only have to go outside to the street and find a few small restaurants. Let's see how it goes without a tour guide. I choose one that looks sort of like a snack bar. A large board shows the pictures of the dishes they serve. They are accompanied by descriptions in Korean, which of course mean nothing to me. Since the person behind the counter doesn't speak a word of English, I have no choice but to look at the pictures and see what other people have on their plates, and then use my hands to indicate what I would like.

The first dish was really something. Various rolls of different lengths and thicknesses swimming in a red sauce, with pieces of a fish cake in it, as I learned after the first bite. The white rolls appear to have been made of rice flour. The texture is very unusual: soft, slightly rubbery, and somehow sticky, but rather lacking in flavor. The really good thing about them is that they soak up the heat! Because even though I smiled when the waiter told me that this dish was "medium hot" (I like my food very spicy) it turned out to be not only one of the hottest dishes I've ever eaten, but also the spiciest thing that I ate on my entire trip to Korea. It was tteokbokki, a popular dish that many street kitchens like to offer for breakfast. You have my full respect, spicy sauce! The fried kimchi rice, which I also ordered, was mellow by contrast and just right for toning down the heat. Then fried tempura — okay, tempura isn't so unusual — with sweet potatoes and zucchini. Then I had what were apparently glass noodles wrapped in a green leaf, something that reminded me of calamari and kimbap (a type of Korean sushi) all dipped in batter and deep fried. The tempura was nice and crispy, just like it should be. For my first meal, that wasn't bad. It tasted pretty good.

Four other tables were occupied in the small, street snack bar. At one of them was seated a group of seven people who were dressed as if they had come straight from work. A gas cooker was placed in the middle of the table with a very hot, heavy saucepan with liquid and noodles on top of it ... I can't exactly see what it is, and I don't want to stare impolitely. Before they start eating, I leave the snack bar and look for the way to the beach.

> Busan is located next to the sea... I have tremendous respect for the water; the sea is a place that always makes me feel at home. The places where I have lived and worked have often been by the water: Portugal, mornings spent watching the waves while drinking a galão (a white coffee) on the beach; Sylt, an island, with water whereever you turn to look. No matter where you are in the world, the sea always flows in the same direction. Its sounds are also the same. That makes it something familiar, which right now I find very comforting.

By chance I happen upon a small market on the way back to my hotel. It has many small aquariums with fresh lobsters, clams, snails, and sea cucumbers. You choose your food, and then they prepare it directly on site. It doesn't get any fresher than that. I notice that at all of these stands only older women are preparing the food — no young women, no men. I'll have to ask the tour guide who will be showing me around later about that. Many young people sit in small groups in the street kitchens separated by plastic sheeting or walls. They laugh, talk, and enjoy the food. There are always a lot of small plates and bowls on the table that are shared among the guests. This is as natural here as eating from your own plate is in Germany.

There are 3.5 million people in Busan — where is everyone at 9:30 p.m. on Friday evening? There's surprisingly little going on in the streets. Maybe it's just in our part of town. I won't be finding that out today because the trip was quite long. I'm really tired, and that slows me down and lessens my curiosity and excitement to discover more.

동그라미 분식

SLEEPLESS IN THE HOTEL – IT IS 5:17 A.M. IN GERMANY. My first meeting with the tour guide is scheduled for 9 a.m. and I have an eventful day ahead of me, but I can't fall asleep. I have so many questions and thoughts running through my head: Can you come to terms with your past, your origins, at some point? Or are you unconsciously always searching? I'm not sure that I have an answer to that or if I will ever find one. But I'm happy to have started my journey. And it's much more than just a journey. I'm not consciously looking for traces from my past. Still, a few weeks ago I wrote a few emails asking if I could possibly visit the "babies home" in Seoul. That's where I stayed for three months before being put up for adoption. Unfortunately, it no longer exists, and the building was demolished. Well, maybe that's how it should be. My husband Christian wasn't sure whether I should really see it, all alone, without him to support me. I don't know. Somehow I think it might have been a place that I could feel a sort of connection to, a place where I had once been brave and strong, yet so small and fragile. I'd avoided taking this trip for so long, but after committing to it, I had started to feel a sense of relief. I was finally doing it. But then, as the trip approached, I started to get nervous. I was completely stressed with anticipation over what I might encounter there. I didn't know what to expect. What would I think of it? Would I like it? What would people there think of me? Would everyone immediately see me as a foreigner? That hasn't been the case. Every person I've met speaks to me in Korean right away. I can't answer even one of their questions, but I'm still glad that they see me as a part of Korea. It puts me at ease and I'm happy that I took this step. I am here.

Day 2, April 7th: Busan. I managed to get a little sleep. Then I met with Hyoung Hwa Heo, our tour guide. Unfortunately, I still can't pronounce her name properly. I asked her if I could call her "Ms. Heo." She said that's okay with her.

In the morning, we visited the Buddhist temple Haedong Yonggungsa. Ms. Heo was born in Busan and is very proud to be able to show me her home city. Our visit to the temple confirms something I had read about in my travel guides; in Korea they place enormous social value on education. Already at a very young age, children are put under incredible pressure to do well in school. That's because in Korea you are only deemed worthy of respect if you have attended one of the best universities. It's not like that in Germany, or at least I've never had the feeling that education is so clearly equated with success or that without an education you're nothing. In Korea, however, it's considered the basis of a successful life, one worthy of admiration. This is reflected in everyday life too and in the way Koreans, young and old, conduct themselves, as my two guides in Busan explained to me (another guide will accompany me in Seoul). And maybe that has something to do with Korean genes. I'm also very determined and only happy once I've achieved my goals, made my wishes come true. Why am I at a temple but suddenly talking about education? That's because it also plays a major role in the temples here, where you can pray for success. One of the many traditions in Korea is that parents take their children to a temple before they have big exams. They place small images of Buddha there in hopes that it will bring their children luck and knowledge. I think this gesture is great. They want to secure the best possible path for their children's future. On the temple grounds, there are also many different statues shaped like different animals, each with a specific meaning. The three most important animals are the dragon, which stands for strength, the turtle for longevity, and the pig for prosperity. Koreans say that the night before a big win, lottery winners have dreamt about a pig.

Within the temple complex, an underground stream flows into a small dark room that's lies beneath the earth. There's also a small Buddha there for good health. You're supposed to pour some of the curative water into a plastic cup and have a drink. There's another small figure outside, under a canopy. Pouring running water over its head three times is supposed to bring good luck. A final bow completes the ritual. There are 108 steps leading to the temple entrance. This is true for every temple. In Buddhism 108 is an important number. Buddha's teachings are summarized in 108 scriptures. And, in the case of the stairs, it's said that each step represents one of the earthly temptations that a person must overcome to achieve nirvana. As they ascend, the seeker's true nature grows lighter and lighter, as they cast off the weight of their suffering. By the time they have reached the temple, the seeker is ready for enlightenment, the stage at which all suffering has disappeared altogether. At the temples, the number 108 is combined with climbing the stairs, a powerful symbol of effort. At another place in the temple complex there's a kind of water basin with two stone bowls below a bridge. If you flip a coin and hit one of these two bowls, they say that your wish will come true.

There are quite a few customs here that are supposed to bring luck. I am not embarking on a study of Buddhism, but I do appreciate that Koreans believe in these things. And Ms. Heo explains that every Korean child goes at least once to the temple with their whole school class, so that every Korean has their own memory of it. This ensures that the tradition truly lives on.

Crab soup and perilla leaves. After the temple, a visit to the Jagalchi Market, Busan's fish market, is on the agenda. Before then, we stop for lunch first at an inn. Many small plates are placed on the table. There's eel and another fried fish. Ms. Heo says it's closely related to mackerel. There's also kimchi; zucchini that's a little paler than bean sprouts in Germany; raw slices of garlic; and green chili peppers. The latter can be quite deceptive; if you pick a "wrong" one, it can be super spicy. There are also two types of white fish sashimi and ssamjang, a thick paste that's also seasoned with fermented fish paste. This creates a sharp, spicy taste that's unusually fishy. When rolled up in the perilla leaves (sesame leaves) along with the roasted eel, however, it's really tasty.

Then there's a crab soup. It's carried to the table in a large pot and placed on a gas cooker. Ah! Something like that was probably what the guests were eating in the restaurant that I visited by myself yesterday. I can see all kinds of vegetables in the soup: onion, leek, green herbs, which continue to cook in the pot at the table.

Even though many foods in Korea are served cold, it's important to always have a hot dish. The soup is ladled into small bowls. Now it's time to work for your meal, because the crab is chopped up very roughly and you have to pull the crab meat from the shells yourself. But it's a lot of fun — and tastes really good.

.

Incredibly effective. Fortified with a good meal, we head to the fish market, which is truly impressive. Some of the sea creatures I encounter there, I've never seen before. I again notice that it's almost exclusively older women (many of whom are probably well over 70), who sit behind the windows and meticulously pour water over clams that are in plastic bowls. With their years of experience, they fillet the fish at breakneck speeds! That sets a whole new benchmark for efficiency in my restaurant. I'll probably have to tell my employees that they are really slow! No! I'm just kidding. I would never do that. But all of these older women are starting to make me wonder what will happen when this generation dies? Who will take over this great fish market and the small food stalls?

Ms. Heo explains that the market opens at 3 a.m. We're there at around noon. By then almost everything has already been sold. But I can still imagine what must have been going on here six hours ago, and I'm glad it's quieter now. The paths between the stands are very narrow so that as many dealers as possible can fit into the covered hall. At most of the stands, you can choose products that are then prepared one floor up in one of the many mini-kitchens and then eaten on site. The thin plastic sheets with elastic bands over the tables are a bit strange; coziness looks different in Korea. But I quickly understand the practical sense behind it. When the guests have all finished eating at a table and have gotten up, the plates are cleared away. You simply grab all four corners of the plastic sheet, fold them up, and the table is clean for the next guests. That's a good thing too because the tables turn over extremely quickly. There's hardly a table that stays empty for more than five minutes. Most German restaurateurs can only dream of such a thing.

You don't have to love everything, but some things you have to love a lot. I see fresh, raw abalone for the first time, a completely new thing for me. It's opened in front of the guests like an oyster, only the abalone has a very firm flesh. The fishmonger cuts it quickly and skillfully into slices. It's followed by another marine creature that's totally new to me: meongge, a sea pineapple that's part of the sea cucumber family. I don't learn more about it until after my return to Germany. If you squeeze the red bump, which has knob-like spines, it spits a jet of water out of an opening. It looks really strange. The rubbery coating is quickly removed with a knife, the thorny exterior is turned inside out, and a yellowish-looking meat emerges, which the fishmonger then cuts into small pieces. The whole process doesn't look very appetizing. I bravely try the abalone first and am very excited. Since it's raw, it's more firm to bite into than I had expected; it has a slightly nutty aroma and tastes a bit like sea salt. Not bad at all! Over the course of my trip I got to try the cooked form of abalone in three differentdishes, in the three different star restaurants. I haveto admit, I've become a bit of an abalone fan, at least in Korea, where it's affordable.

Meongge and I, however, are unlikely to become friends. Under most circumstances, I'm not a squeamish eater. That said, I have to muster up a lot of courage to swallow the yellowish flesh. It's soft and slippery, and I bite off only a tiny piece. That's enough for me. I don't care for the bitter taste and consistency, but I'm here to try as many things as possible that you can (only) get in Korea.

Strolling through the market. After lunch we head to the Haeundae Market. It has several stands that sell a huge variety of kimchis. Not only cabbage, but a wide range of vegetables like radish, Chinese cabbage, Swiss chard, and others that I don't immediately recognize that are pickled as kimchi. Later, I learn from my guide in Seoul, Jain, that there's even a kimchi holiday in Korea. That's when the family gets together and pickles mountains of kimchi. Because it preserves well, they have enough for the family and ready as a gift when they visit friends.

Even though I don't have much of a "sweet tooth," today I decide to try a sweet dumpling fried in a lot of fat. I was intrigued by the long line of locals at a stand where they were making them. The dumpling is filled with sunflower seeds and sprinkled with sugar and a little cinnamon. It's pretty tasty. I understand why there's a line. I notice corn at another food stand. It's ripe but looks a little like a lighter version of corn in Germany. Next to it, yellow corn would look as if someone had painted it. To wash down the dumpling, I try a rice drink that you can use for cooking but that can also be drunk straight. It's chilled, slightly sweet, and refreshing.

After the market we go back to the hotel for a little while. Tonight should be exciting: We're having dinner in the fugu restaurant.

Eat fugu – and die? At home in Germany, I'd seen in my itinerary that we were going to visit a fugu restaurant. Fugu! Isn't that the puffer fish that only specially trained cooks are allowed to prepare? Otherwise, there's the risk that the meal may end in death?! Okay! I want to try as much as possible, and I trust the people who organized this trip. They surely wouldn't want to lose their customers. We enter a very large restaurant with tables that are packed with guests. Only two or three of them are occupied by couples. Seated at the other tables are mostly larger groups that are obviously having fun. The noise level is correspondingly loud. I noticed that during my first evening in Korea: Dining out here is always a communal experience.

Luckily, the menu has pictures. I'm glad for that too because that means I can understand it better. Yet, it also makes me wonder if this place is pretty touristy? Then I consider the fact that there aren't that many Western tourists in Korea and I don't always recognize the Asian ones. Plus, Koreans travel within their own country and are then tourists themselves. Pushing these thoughts aside, we order three dishes: "Bokguk-Fugu Soup," "Spicy Fugu Skin," and "Bulgogi Style Fugu." The latter interests me the most, because we have a dish on the menu at Yoso called "Bulgogi Style Mackerel."

No sooner has the order been placed than the server fills the table with lots of small bowls of banchan (Korean sidedishes): tofu with red chili paste, green onions, and sesame. I prefer my tofu this way: two types of seaweed, fish cake, spicy radishes and sour radishes, rice, and soybean stock with seaweed. Next up are the fugu entrees. The first one is a plate with fugu skin in a spicy red sauce. The whole thing looks a bit like a "devil's salad" (which I remember from my childhood as a salad made from peppers, beef, onions, and cayenne pepper). In terms of taste, this dish is very different and spicy. And when I say spicy here, I mean spicy. Really spicy. The sight of the skin takes some getting used to, so it takes some effort to try it. It's raw and quite thick. On some strips of skin you can even spot the porcupine-like quills that you can see when the fugu is swimming in the tank. But why not?! I taste it. And there it is again, that consistency that Koreans love, as Ms. Heo informs me, but which I still have to get used to. This skin is not quite as rubbery as the rice cake pieces last night, but is it necessarily better …? I nibble my way through the other bowls before I dare to try it again. But it doesn't really get any better.

The pufferfish soup (or bokguk) is good. Like many dishes in Korea, people say that it's rich in vitamins and good for hangovers. The bokguk is served, as many Korean dishes often are, in a heavy, cast-iron pot. This keeps it warm for a long time. The clear fish broth is simmering and bubbling away. It has a few bite-size pieces of fugu as well as chopped cabbage and other green leaves and stems floating in it. There's a bundle of enoki mushrooms lying on top of it. The fugu meat is white and rather firm; it has very little fat. It doesn't seem to have a strong flavor of its own.

The bulgogi-style fugu looks very appealing: It has bean sprouts, green beans, and another bunch of white enoki mushrooms, some chives, and white sesame seeds. The appearance of the dish is important in Korea. In terms of taste, it goes in a completely different direction than the marinade I use for my dish at Yoso. The Korean version features grilled slices of fish tossed in a red, spicy chili paste. The meat is rather firm, so it doesn't disintegrate when frying. It tastes like chili paste and is quite spicy.

This ends my first full day in Korea. Tomorrow we're heading to Gyeongju, the former capital, which is now a rather small city with just under 300,000 inhabitants. First, I have to digest my impressions and my first culinary experiences…

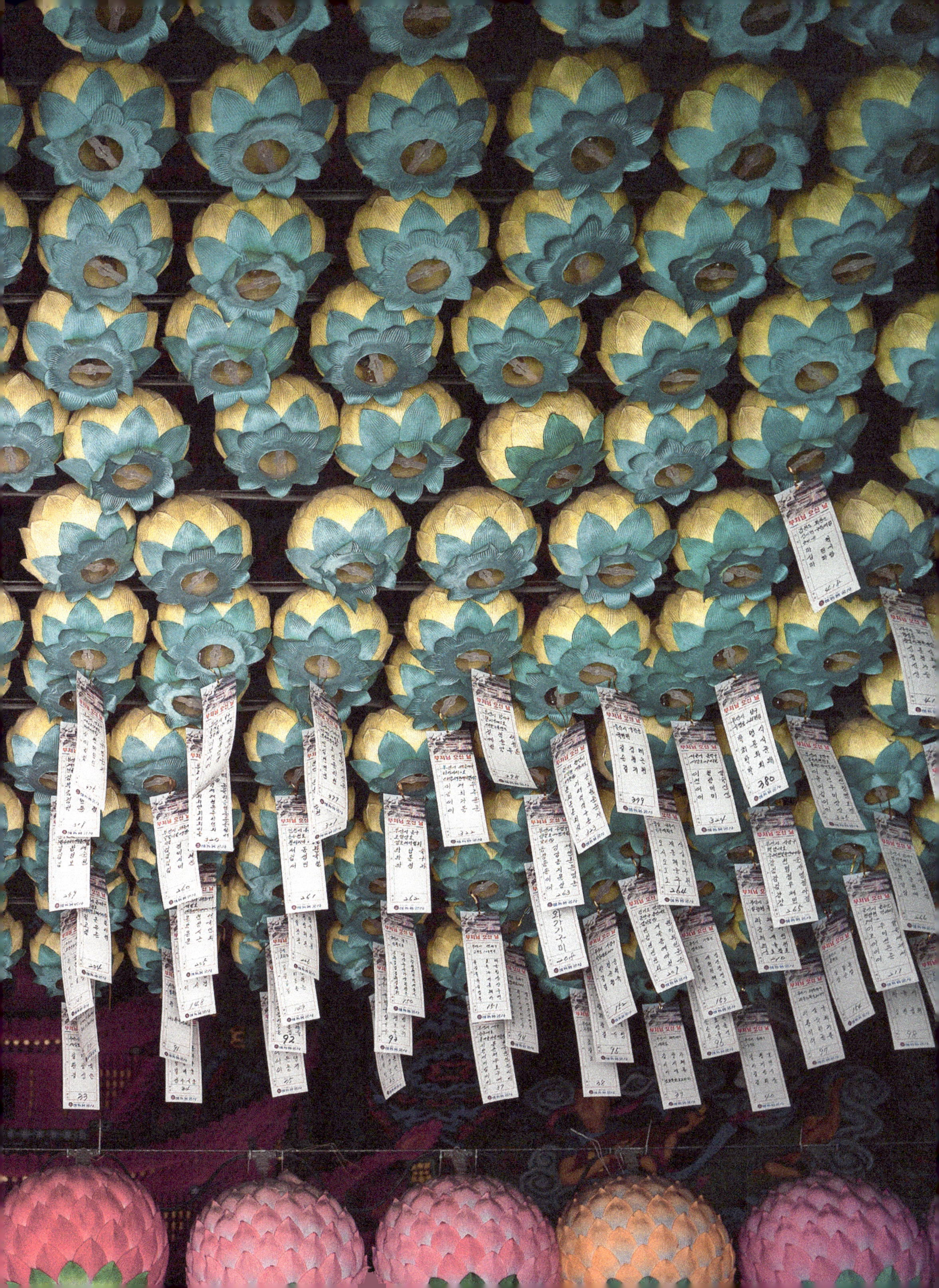

Kimbap
Rice rolls

김밥

Serves 4 | Prep time: **90 minutes**

For the kimbap
4 cups (750 g) freshly
  cooked rice
Salt
6 teaspoons toasted
  sesame oil
8 cups (250 g) fresh
  spinach
3 cloves garlic
1 large carrot
3 teaspoons neutral
  vegetable oil
½ lb (250 g) beef
  tenderloin or fillet
2 teaspoons soy sauce
Freshly ground black
  pepper
1 tablespoon brown sugar
  Neutral vegetable oil
3 eggs
5 sheets kim (roasted
  seaweed sheets)
5 strips of yellow pickled
  daikon radish (danmuji)
6 tsp sesame oil, plus some
  for the knife
Salt and pepper

To serve
Soy sauce
Pickled ginger

Kimbap
Place the freshly cooked rice into a bowl, season with a little salt and 2 teaspoons of toasted sesame oil, and mix with a wooden spoon. Set the rice aside to cool.

For the filling, clean and sort through the spinach. Quickly blanch the spinach in boiling water and drain well. Peel and mince two cloves of garlic. Mix the lightly squeezed spinach with the garlic, ½ teaspoon salt, and 2 teaspoons toasted sesame oil and set aside. Peel and julienne the carrots. Mix the julienned carrots with ¼ teaspoon of salt and let sit for 10 minutes. Heat 1 teaspoon of vegetable oil in a pan. Sauté the well-drained carrot strips for 1 minute, then remove them from the pan and set aside.

Cut the beef into thin strips. Peel and mince the last clove of garlic. Place the meat strips into a bowl with the garlic, soy sauce, a little pepper, brown sugar, and 2 teaspoons of roasted sesame oil, mix well, and marinate for 30 minutes. Then heat 1 teaspoon of vegetable oil in a pan. Pour the meat strips and marinade into the pan and stir fry until cooked. Remove from heat and set aside.

Create an omelet from the eggs. To make the omelet, heat 1 teaspoon oil in a non-stick pan. Beat the eggs with ¼ teaspoon salt and add to the pan and cook one minute. Using a heatproof silicone spatula, gently lift the cooked eggs from the edges of the pan and tilt the pan to allow the uncooked eggs to flow to the edges. Heat for a few more seconds, fold the omelet in half and slide onto a cutting board. Cut the omelet into strips and set aside.

To finish, place a seaweed sheet with the shiny side up, on a bamboo mat. Evenly spread one-fifth of the rice on the seaweed, leaving a strip about 1"-wide at the top. Arrange one-fifth of each of the spinach, carrots, meat strips, egg strips, and a strip of yellow daikon radish in neat horizontal rows over the entire width of the seaweed.

Beginning on the side nearest you, roll the bamboo mat up and over the fillings. Use firm but gentle pressure to hold the ingredients in place. Moisten the top edge of the seaweed with cold water to seal the roll. Repeat the steps with the rest of the ingredients to make four more rolls. Coat the blade of a very sharp knife with a little sesame oil and slice the five rolls into bite-size pieces.

To serve
Arrange the sliced rice rolls side by side on a plate. Serve with the soy sauce and pickled ginger.

Tteokbokki
Rice Cakes in a Spicy Sauce

떡볶이

Serves 4 | Prep time: 50 minutes

For the tteokbokki
5 dried anchovies or
   shiitake mushrooms
1 piece of kombu (dried
   kelp, measuring about 4"
   x 4")
1 tablespoon gochujang
   (spicy Korean chili paste)
1 teaspoon gochugaru
   (Korean chili flakes)
1 tablespoon sugar
1–2 tablespoons dark soy
   sauce
1 tablespoon maple sugar
1 bunch green onions
1 lb (500 g) tteok (rod-
   shaped rice cakes)
8 oz (250 g) eomuk (Korean
   fish cakes)
4 eggs, hardboiled and
   peeled

Tteokbokki
Place anchovies and kombu in a pan with a high rim. Add 3 cups of water, bring to a boil and simmer uncovered for 15 minutes so that some liquid can evaporate. Pass the resulting stock through a fine-mesh strainer into a bowl. (The anchovies and kombu are no longer needed.) Pour it back into the pan. Mix in the spice paste, chili pepper flakes, sugar, soy sauce, and maple syrup. Stir thoroughly.

Rinse the green onions. Set one aside and cut the rest of the green onions into 1"-pieces.

Add the rice cakes, fish cakes, green onions, and peeled eggs to the stock and simmer uncovered for 15–20 minutes, stirring occasionally, until it is soft and creamy. Be careful to make sure that the eggs stay whole. Finely chop the remaining green onion.

To serve
Transfer the rice cakes with one egg each onto deep plates and garnish with the chopped green onions.

TIP

Kombu (also known as kelp or dasima) is a brown algae that grows in cold, clear waters around the world. Kombu has a slightly fishy taste that, depending on where it comes from, can be either mild and sweet (Asia) or rather strong (Europe). .

Baechu kimchi
Napa cabbage kimchi

배추김치

Makes about 4 ½ lb (2 kg) of kimchi | Prep time: 60 minutes | Marinating time: 6 hours plus 7 days

For the Baechu kimchi

1 head of Napa or Chinese
  cabbage (approx. 3-3 ½ lb
  / 1.5 kg)
½ cup (150 g) salt
2 tablespoons rice flour
2 tablespoons brown sugar
5 cloves garlic
1 small onion
1 teaspoon freshly grated
  ginger ¼ cup (50 g)
  gochugaru (Korean chili
  pepper flakes)
1/3 cup (75 mL) fish sauce
3 cups (400 g) daikon
  radish
1 ½ cups (200 g) carrots
2 ½ cups (300 g) Asian
  pears
1 bunch green onions
1 bunch garlic chives
  (Chinese chives)
2 tablespoons saeujeot
  (fermented shrimp)

Baechu kimchi

Carefully cut the Napa cabbage in half so that the leaves remain as intact as possible. Gently rinse the halves. Fill a large pot with water and immerse the halves in it so that the Napa cabbage is completely covered with water. Remove cabbage from the pot of water and let drain. Rub each individual layer of cabbage on both sides with salt, adding more to the thick white parts near the stems. Place the cabbage halves in another large bowl and brine for 6 hours. Rotate cabbage every two hours and pour the salty water that forms over the Napa cabbage to cover it. After the brining period is complete, remove from large bowl and thoroughly rinse the Napa cabbage under cold water to remove the salt. Quarter it and drain well in a colander.

For the kimchi paste, measure out 1 cup water. Take out 3 tablespoons of water from the 1 cup and put it in a bowl, stir in the rice flour and sugar until smooth and combine with the rest of the water. Bring this mixture to a boil in a saucepan and simmer for about 5 minutes. Once it reaches a pudding-like consistency, remove from heat and refrigerate until cool.

Peel and finely chop the garlic and onion. Mix the garlic, onion, ginger, chili pepper flakes, and fish sauce into the cooled paste. Peel and julienne the radish and carrots. Cut out the core of the Asian pears and julienne the flesh. Rinse the green onions and thinly slice the white parts. Clean, dry, and chiffonade the garlic chives. Add the vegetables, the fermented shrimp, and the seasoning paste to a bowl and mix well.

Place the drained cabbage on a platter and toss the cabbage with the marinade, coating well. (Note: be sure to wear disposable plastic gloves.) Transfer the cabbage to clean, large glass jars with lids that fit snugly and place the jars in a cool, dark, and dry space. After about 2 days, the kimchi should be fermented and smell sour.

You can now put the kimchi in the refrigerator and allow it to ferment another 5-7 days. The kimchi can then either be eaten immediately or continue to ferment (no more than 2 months). You can taste it occasionally to determine when the kimchi has reached your desired taste.

이곳 가게의 상인 60~70%는 반찬을 직접
만든다. 가게 안쪽에는 반찬을 만드느라 바쁘
게 움직이는 상인들의 모습을 쉽게 볼 수 있
다. 공장 등 다른 곳에서 배송되는
반찬으로는 주로 ... 수 ...
었다고한다.
직접 만들기 때문에 ...
다. 하루 판매 ... 가게를
회원이다.
실제로 2일 ... 확인한 결과 ...
... 적은 ...
... 고기 ...

상현제	
무말랭이	국내산
각무기	국내산
맥반젓갈	러시아산
창란젓갈	러시아산
낙지젓갈	영덕국산
동치미	중국산
오이김치	영덕국산
	국내산
배추김치	국내산
총각김치	국내산
영념게장	국내산
공입깻잎	국내산
갓 물김치	국내산
고추젓갈	중국산
얼무짜박이	국내산

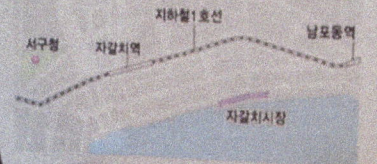

서구청 · 자갈치역 · 지하철1호선 · 남포동역

자갈치시장

... 등지에도 단골 손님들이 많다. 택배 주문
... 가능하다.
... 김치 반 포기 5천원이며 나머지 반찬은 고객
... 원하는 만큼 소량으로도 판매한다.

... 입 전 시식하며 신선도 체크

...핑팁=반찬은 뭐니뭐니해도 맛과 신선
...고다. 사고 싶은 반찬이 있으면 구입
...시 시식해보자. 끝 맛이 짭짤하고 개운
...선한 반찬 쉰 맛이 ...
...가능성이 높 ...

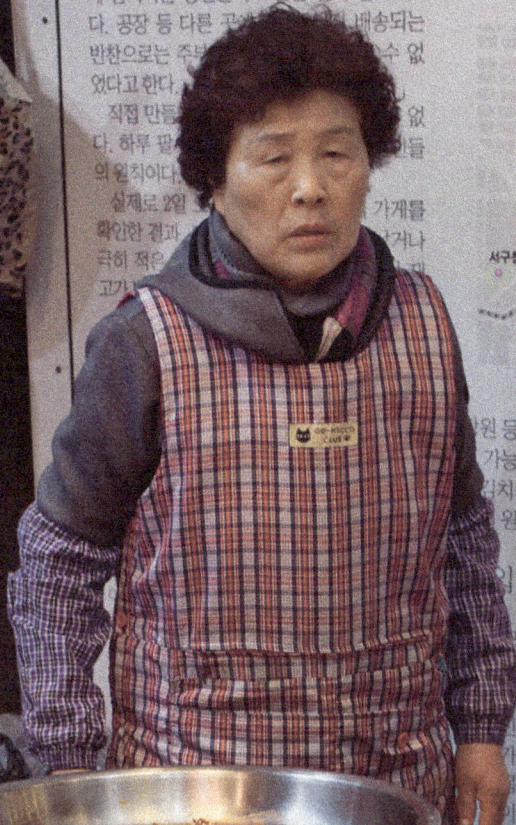

Kimchi Bokkeumbap
Kimchi Fried Rice

김치 볶음밥

Serves 4 | Prep time: **30 minutes**

For the Kimchi bokkeumbap:

2 tablespoons white sesame
   seeds
2 ½ cups (350 g) kimchi
   with juice (see "Baechu
   kimchi – Napa cabbage
   kimchi" recipe on page 32)
2 tablespoons neutral
   vegetable oil 1-2
   tablespoons gochujang
   (spicy
Korean chili paste)
2 tablespoons soy sauce
3 cups (600 g) cooked
   sushi rice (from day
   before)
1-2 tablespoons toasted
   sesame oil
Salt
Freshly ground black
   pepper
4 green onions
4 eggs

To serve

8 sheets kim (roasted
   seaweed sheets)
4 eggs

Kimchi bokkeumbap

Toast the sesame seeds in a non-stick pan, without oil, then let cool. Using a fine-mesh strainer, drain kimchi, reserving the juice. Mix the kimchi liquid (or use kimchi juice) with the gochujang and soy sauce. Heat 1 tablespoon of vegetable oil in a pan. Sauté the drained kimchi for a few minutes until it is slightly caramelized. In a small bowl, mix the reserved kimchi juice, gochujang and soy sauce, and set it aside. Add the prepared sauce and rice to the pan with the kimchi and stir fry until thoroughly mixed, about 3 minutes. Season to taste with the sesame oil, salt and pepper. Heat remaining the vegetable oil in a sauté pan, add eggs and fry for 3 minutes. Flip and fry 2-3 minutes more, until egg whites are cooked and yolk is slightly runny.

To serve

Rinse the green onions and cut into thin rings. In a separate bowl, crumble the roasted seaweed leaves. Arrange the fried rice in deep plates. Place a fried egg on top and sprinkle with plenty of crumbled seaweed and chopped green onions.

TIP

Sometimes the fried rice may require more liquid than others. If the kimchi you are using is rather dry, you can supplement the liquid with kimchi juice. You can order kimchi juice on the Internet.

Kkotgetang
Crab Stew

꽃 게 장

Serves 4 | Prep time: **45 minutes**

For the kkotgetang:

1 lb (500 g) blue crab (fresh
  or frozen)
6 dried anchovies
7 oz (20 g) dried shrimp
2 teaspoons gochugaru
  (Korean chili flakes)
1 tablespoon gochujang
  (spicy Korean chili paste)
1 tablespoon doenjang
  (Korean fermented
  soybean paste)
2 tablespoons guk-ganjang
  (lighter Korean soy sauce)
1 tablespoon fish sauce
1 ¼ cups (150 g) daikon
  radish
1 small zucchini
2 green onions
1 red chili pepper
3 cloves garlic
1 bunch chrysanthemum
  greens (watercress also
  works)
Freshly ground black
  pepper

To serve
Cooked rice

Kkotgetang

Peel the blue crabs and cut off the heads. Set aside the crab meat. If necessary, remove the heads and viscera from the anchovies. Place the blue crab shells and heads and the rinsed anchovies and dried shrimp in a large pot. Add 1 quart of water and bring to a boil. Let the stock simmer for about 15 minutes. Pour the stock through a fine-mesh strainer into a second pot.

To make the seasoning paste, combine the chili flakes, chili powder, soybean paste, soy sauce, and fish sauce. Stir the seasoning paste into the hot stock. Rinse the radish and zucchini and cut into thin slices. Rinse, trim the root end, and finely chop the green onions. Clean the chili peppers, remove the seeds, and finely chop. Peel and mince the garlic. Add the radish slices and crab meat to the stock and simmer for about 10 minutes, until the radish slices are almost soft. Add the zucchini slices, green onion, chili pepper, and garlic and let the soup simmer for another 3 minutes.

Clean the chrysanthemum greens and discard the thick stems. Season the soup with pepper and add the chrysanthemum greens.

To serve
Ladle the soup into deep soup bowls. Serve the rice in a separate bowl.

江

GYEONGJU

The capital of
the ancient
kingdom
of Silla

Day 3, April 8th. From Busan to Gyeongju. In the morning we head out of the city and then onto the highway. And because the coffee in the hotel was pretty weak, we stop at the nearest gas station along route. I need a strong cup of coffee in the morning to get my day off to a good start.

Drinking coffee is popular in Korea. That really surprised me. I thought the main drink here would be tea, but, as I found out, that completely changed a few years ago. Today, you see a lot of people walking around with a "coffee to go" cup in hand. Speaking of "to go" cups, Korean cities have very few trash cans.

Garbage has to be carefully sorted and put in bags in specified locations in front of the house door. Every bag that's picked up costs about 50 cents or 1 dollar — that's a lot of money. If you violate these rules, the fines are quite high. The upshot is that the cities look very clean, especially compared to other major cities around the world. It's possible that we simply didn't visit dirtier areas. Still, I can't figure out where all the garbage goes.

In any case, after the coffee break, we continue towards Gyeongju in southeast Korea and stop briefly before today's first destination: Seokguram Grotto. Ms. Heo points to a mountain where you can see the outline of a temple at the top. There, way up high, is Seokguram Grotto. A very winding path leads to the parking lot in front of the entrance to the grotto. Since it's Sunday and the sun is shining, there are a lot of visitors. Most of them appear to be Korean. There are relatively few European tourists as it is, at least I hardly see any on my trip. Fortunately, I don't attract any attention at all: I am one of them. Somehow that always makes me feel good.

History and memories. There is a small path, decorated with colored lanterns, leading to Seokguram Grotto. Some people may find it kitschy, but I like it. I think it's beautiful. Despite the large number of visitors, the atmosphere is relaxed and in some way spiritual. Construction of the artificial grotto began in 751 and was completed in 774. It is one of South Korea's national treasures and, along with the Bulguksa Temple, which we will also visit, is a UNESCO World Heritage site. The Seokguram Grotto is home to the famous statue of the Buddha that is nearly 12-feet tall and is now protected under a concrete dome. It was carved from a single block of stone in 774. You're not allowed to take photographs here. That's a good thing too; it shows respect to the Buddhist faith. You don't always have to take pictures to capture the moment. You can feel the power radiating from the place. This memory is enough for me. Go to Seokguram Grotto and experience it for yourself: You will know what I mean.

Outside the grotto we enjoy the magnificent view of the valley and the east coast of Korea. Then it's back down the mountain to Bulguksa Temple. There are even more visitors here than in the grotto. The complex extends over a much larger area. They have the same colorful lanterns. Some of them have notes attached where visitors have written their wishes. I think this custom is great! I hope that every single wish that has been immortalized here will come true.

Ms. Heo observes that elementary school children visit the Bulguska Temple and learn about its history. Koreans take a lot of pride in knowing about their country and its past. And when the students return to Bulguksa Temple everyone has their own memories of it. Ms. Heo says that when she was a child, the roads were not as well developed and that the access road to the temple was much narrower and more dangerous. These memories may be little things, but they make life unique. I'm feeling happy that in every moment I'm allowed to spend here, I learn a bit more about the life and traditions of this country.

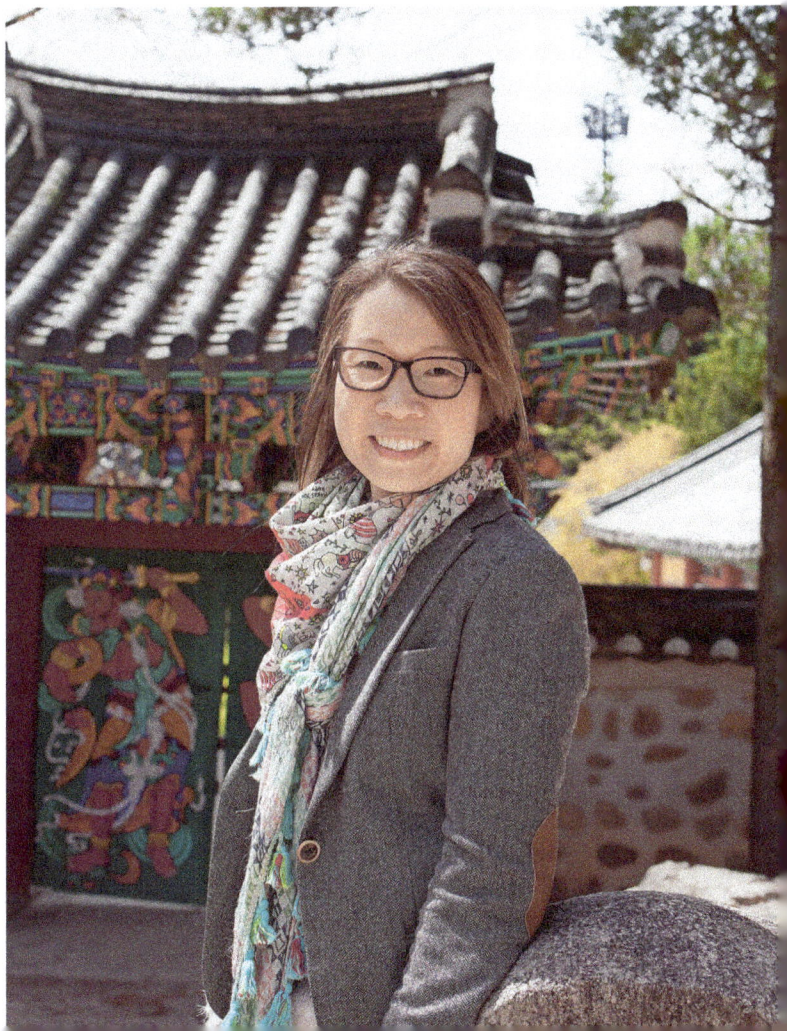

Lunch with daetongbap. After our visit to these two very impressive sites in Gyeongju, lunch is next on the itinerary. As Ms. Heo explains, every region of Korea has its specialty. The specialty here is daetongbap, a kind of meatball made from beef or pork. Within a few minutes, we arrive at a restaurant where you don't need to make a reservation because of the unique way that they assign tables after the guests arrive. Ms. Heo asks for a table and receives a slip of paper with a number on it. As soon as a table is available, they announce a number over a loudspeaker. As a chef, I think this is a bad idea. It makes the restaurant feel like an assembly line.

You can order beef, pork or pork and beef daetongbap here. I choose pork and beef. As always, the many other small "side dishes" (banchan) are put on the table first. We start with a kimchi pancake, a kind of baked crêpe with finely chopped kimchi, followed by a black bean soup with tofu and green onions. They bring out more small bowls containing kimchi with tofu, green onions with red chili paste, lotus root in yuzu syrup, and small salty fish with peanuts. You can, by the way, find these little fish in many restaurants, and they are pretty good for seasoning. We are then served pear slices covered with white cream in a bowl. At first, I couldn't discern the ingredients in this dish correctly, but then I notice that the pears add a fruity-sweet taste to the food, which is also needed to mellow it. There are lettuce leaves again, this time Lollo Rosso, which are topped with a piece of roast beef or pork coated with the ssamjang paste and combined with a little rice. I try very hard to elegantly get the whole thing in my mouth.

Since it drips a lot, I quickly notice that I'm not really able to do this. All the others are going through the same thing, but perhaps just a little more skillfully.

The raw crab, which is marinated with red chili paste, is a delicacy and not very cheap. I have to smile. This dish could be the equivalent for the Koreans of eating crawdads for Americans, because you "suck" the raw crab meat from the shell. The resulting taste is a combination of the slight sweetness of the raw crab meat (which has a very unusual consistency) and the spiciness of the paprika paste. I'm not quite sure yet whether this will be one of my favorite dishes. In general, the consistencies and temperatures are very different from what I know from Germany. For example, I try to always include something crunchy in my dishes to keep the mouthfeel exciting. There are also very crunchy vegetables here from time to time, and a lot of the food is served cold, arranged separately in bowls, and then combined and eaten together according to individual taste. As I mentioned before, there's always a warm or even hot dish, often a soup. Since the many small bowls are all placed on the table at the same time, the cold temperature is an advantage. And there's something else about Korean culinary culture that I find interesting; many dishes are linked with good health. For example, the seaweed soup we were served today is eaten mainly by pregnant women after giving birth, often to clean their blood. But there's no meaning behind our being served this soup today; they served it to my male photographer too.

Surrounded by tombs and ponds. Ms. Heo often draws my attention to things that I've never thought about in Germany. This time the occasion is the Daereungwon Tomb Complex, which is our next destination. The ancient kings and their families from different dynasties were buried here in man- made hills and that's what leads us to talking about funerals. Because in Korea people think about where they, or their ashes, will be interred. Due to the lack of space, most people are cremated. When I explain that there are large cemeteries in every town in Germany and that many people are even buried in coffins, Ms. Heo is astonished.

In the evening we drive to the Anapji Pond, formerly known as Wolji, which means "pond reflecting the moon." It's a beautiful complex that used to be part of a palace. The light reflects on the surface of the water, especially at this time of day, and makes the place appear mystical. The shoreline is designed in such a way that you can't see the entire pond from any point and it appears to be endless, as if you were looking out over a vast ocean. There's a miniature representation of the palace in one of the covered buildings near the shore. This gives visitors an idea of what once stood here during the Silla Kingdom.

There's a lot going on here, and once again I notice that Koreans (and Asian tourists?) really like taking photos. I wonder if the selfie generation originated here in Korea, because two large cell phone manufacturers have their headquarters here. Nearly everyone here is taking a selfie, and everyone is obviously having a lot of fun. And when they pose for their picture, everyone makes two signs with their fingers. I know about the V sign with the index finger and middle finger, but Ms. Heo points out that Koreans also interlace their index finger and thumb so that the fingertips form a heart.

My first bibimbap. We go out to dinner a little later than usual. That is probably why we're almost the only guests in the restaurant, which consists of small, self-contained rooms. The rooms have low tables where you can sit cross-legged on the floor.

The restaurant is serving bibimbap, which is one of the most popular Korean dishes. It comes, as you would expect, with lots of small bowls filled with kimchi, bok choy, tofu, and a kind of pancake made from the green part of the green onion and green pepper. We're also served a bowl of rice that has been dyed yellow with a flower "capsule" but does not have a strong flavor of its own. The special bibimbap vegetables are nicely arranged in the bowl: bean sprouts, zucchini, strips of fried egg, green vegetables, beech mushrooms, spinach, and nori leaves and sesame seeds on top. I mix everything together, including the yellow rice and chili paste. Later on, when I'm in Seoul, my tour guide, Jain, teaches me how to do it properly. What stands out here, though, is just how delicious vegetarian food can be. I don't miss meat at all.

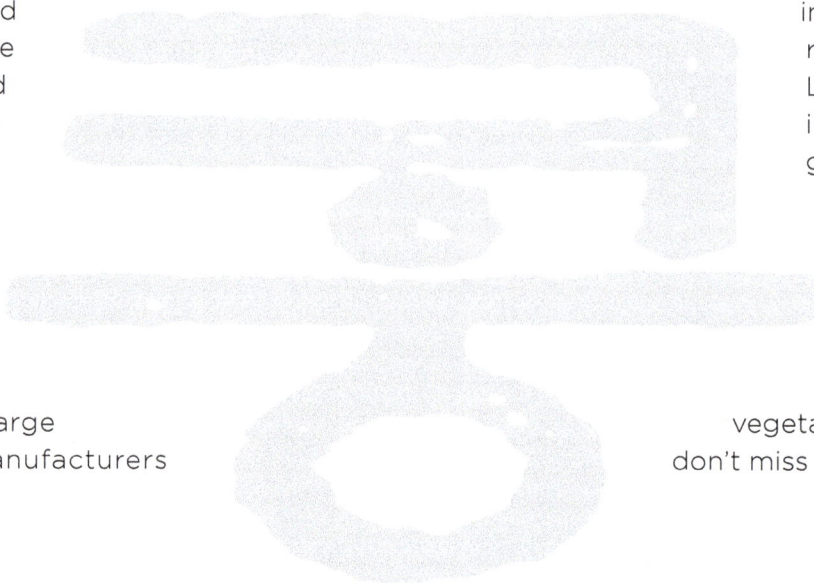

Ssamjang
(Korean Chili Paste)

쌈장

Makes approx. ½ cup (150 g) | Prep time: **10 minutes**

For the ssamjang
1 tablespoon white sesame
  seeds
2 cloves garlic
1 onion
2 green onions
5 tablespoons doenjang
  (Korean fermented
  soybean paste)
3 1/2 tablespoons
  gochujang (spicy Korean
  chili paste)
1 tablespoon sugar or liquid
  honey
1 tablespoon toasted
  sesame oil
1 1/2 tablespoon Korean rice
  syrup
1 tablespoon finely chopped
  green chili pepper

Ssamjang
Toast the sesame seeds in a non-stick pan, without oil. Peel and finely chop the garlic and onion. Rinse and trim the root end, and finely chop the green onions. Mix the remaining ingredients in a bowl until the sugar has dissolved.

Ssamjang paste can be used either immediately or can be stored in small freezer containers for up to a month. Ssamjang is typically served with salad or Chinese cabbage leaves as a spicy side dish to meat or vegetables. No Korean kitchen is complete without at least some Ssamjang in it.

Kimchi Jeon
Kimchi Pancake

김치전

Serves 4 | Prep time: **30 minutes**

For the Kimchi jeon
1 onion
2 cups (300 g) kimchi (see
  "Baechu kimchi" on p. 32)
5 tablespoons kimchi liquid
  (see "Baechu kimchi" on p.
  32)
Salt
1 teaspoon sugar
2 cups (240 g) cake flour
4 tablespoons grape seed
  oil

Kimchi jeon
Peel and finely chop the onion. Chop the kimchi. Mix the chopped onion and kimchi together with the kimchi liquid and a pinch of salt and sugar in a bowl. Sift the flour over it, add ½ cup of water and combine the mixture into a wet dough.

Preheat the oven to 400°F. Heat the oil in a non-stick pan. Pour 1/4 of the batter into the pan with a ladle. Evenly distribute the batter over the surface of the pan and cook the pancake over medium heat until the underside is golden brown and crispy. Flip pancake and continue cooking until the other side is golden brown. Cook three more pancakes from the remaining batter. Keep the pancakes warm in preheated oven until ready to serve.

To serve
Arrange the pancakes on plates and serve.

Doenjang Jjigae
Fermented Soybean Paste Stew

된 장 찌 개

Serves 4 | Prep time: 50 minutes

for the doenjang jjigae

1 bunch green onions
2 cloves garlic
1 onion
¼ cup (20 g) fresh ginger
5 dried anchovies
2 sheets dried seaweed
3 dried shiitake mushrooms
1 teaspoon black
  peppercorns
1 tablespoon neutral
  vegetable oil
3 1/2 tablespoons doenjang
  (fermented Korean
  soybean paste)
1 zucchini
3 ½ oz (100 g) oyster
  mushrooms
9 oz (250 g) medium firm
  tofu
1 fresh green chili pepper
1 tablespoon toasted
  sesame oil
1 tablespoon soy sauce

Doenjang jjigae

For the broth, rinse three of the green onions. Peel the garlic, onion, and ginger. Roughly chop and add them to a large saucepan. Remove the heads and viscera from the dried anchovies. Add the seaweed, mushrooms, peppercorns, and rinsed anchovies to the pot. Add 2 quarts of water. Bring the liquid to a boil and simmer for about 30 minutes, then pour the broth through a fine-mesh strainer. You will need about 2 ½ cups of the broth.

Heat the vegetable oil in a saucepan. Fry the soybean paste briefly in it and stir it with a little hot stock until smooth, then pour in the remaining stock (just under 2 ½ cups). Bring the stew to a boil. Rinse the zucchini and mushrooms, cut into small pieces and add to the stew. Chop the tofu into cubes and add to the stew. Clean the chili peppers, remove the seeds, and chop into fine rings. Add the chili peppers with the sesame oil to the stew and briefly bring to a boil. Season with soy sauce to taste.

To serve

Ladle the hot stew into deep bowls and serve with ssamjang and lettuce leaves.

Dubu Kimchi
Tofu With Stir-Fried Cabbage Kimchi

두부김치

Serves 4 | Prep time: 30 minutes

For the Dubu kimchi
1 tablespoon white sesame
  seeds
2 green onions
1 onion
4 cloves garlic
2 tablespoons gochujang
  (spicy Korean chili paste)
1 tablespoon gochugaru
  (Korean chili flakes)
2 tablespoons soy sauce
2 1 tablespoon rice syrup
3 cups (400 g) kimchi with
  juice (see "Baechu kimchi"
  on p. 32)
Neutral vegetable oil
1 tablespoon toasted
  sesame oil
Salt
Freshly ground black
  pepper
16 oz (500 g) firm tofu

Dubu kimchi
Toast the sesame seeds in a non-stick pan, without oil. Rinse the green onions and cut into thin slices. Peel the onion and garlic and dice very finely.

For the seasoning mixture, mix the chili paste, chili flakes, soy sauce, and rice syrup together thoroughly. Cut the kimchi into small pieces. Heat the oil in a pan. Stir-fry the kimchi with the stock and seasoning mixture for about 7 minutes, stirring constantly. Then add the onion, green onions, and garlic and fry for another 3 minutes. Stir in the sesame oil.

Season the vegetables with salt and pepper. Boil around 4 ½ cups of water in a saucepan and place the tofu block in it. Cook the tofu for about 2 minutes. Remove tofu from water, drain well and cut into cubes.

To serve
Divide the tofu cubes on four plates and spoon stir-fried kimchi on top.

Variation with meat
Cut 5 oz (150 g) of raw pork belly into 1/8" bite-size slices and marinate with the seasoning mix.

Heat the oil in the pan. Stir-fry the marinated pork vigorously for about 30 minutes, then add the kimchi. Prepare the tofu as described above and finish the dish in the same way.

Variation with fish
Drain 1 can of tuna in its own juice through a fine-mesh strainer and cook it in a pan with the kimchi, then finish as described above. Prepare the tofu as described above and finish the dish in the same way.

Neobiani
Marinated Grilled Beef

너비아니

Serves 4 | Prep time: 30 minutes | Marinating time: 10 minutes plus 40 minutes

For the neobiani
1 lb (600 g) beef tenderloin
1 medium Asian pear
1 clove of garlic
1 green onion
1 tablespoon freshly grated
   ginger
5 tablespoons soy sauce
3 tablespoons sugar
1 tablespoon liquid honey
1 tablespoon sesame salt
1/2 teaspoon freshly ground
black pepper
2 tablespoons toasted
   sesame oil
1 tablespoon neutral
   vegetable oil

To serve
Ssamjang (see "Ssamjang"
   recipe on page 54)
Lettuce leaves

Neobiani
Pat the meat dry, then cut against the grain into thin slices. Peel and core the pears and grate the flesh very finely. Arrange the meat slices on a plate and spread the grated pear evenly over them. Marinate the meat for 10 minutes.

For the seasoning sauce, mince the garlic. Rinse, trim the root end, and finely chop the green onions. In a small bowl, combine the garlic, green onion, ginger, soy sauce, sugar, honey, sesame salt, pepper, and sesame oil until the sugar and honey have dissolved. Brush the meat with the sauce and let it sit for 30 minutes.

Preheat the grill and brush the grate with a little oil. Place the meat on the grate and grill for about 2-3 minutes on each side.

To serve
Arrange the grilled meat on plates and serve with ssamjang and lettuce leaves.

TIP

The beef in the photo was minced and then marinated.

Sundubu Jjigae
Stew with Tofu and Seafood

순두부찌개

Serves 4 | Prep time: 50 minutes

For the sundubu jjigae

7 dried anchovies
¾ cup (100 g) daikon radish
2 green onions
1 sheet dried kelp (seaweed, approx. 4" x 4")
1 garlic clove
1 tablespoon neutral vegetable oil
1 tablespoon gochugaru (Koreanchili flakes)
1/2 tablespoon soy sauce
Freshly ground black pepper
1 lb (500 g) mixed seafood (calamari, shrimp, clams)
2 oz (50 g) oyster mushrooms
2 small shiitake mushrooms
12 oz (350 g) silken tofu
2 eggs
1 teaspoon toasted sesame oil
Salt

To serve

2 green onions

Sundubu jjigae

If needed, remove the heads and viscera of the anchovies. Peel and finely chop the radish. Rinse, trim the root end, and roughly chop the green onions. In a large saucepan add the rinsed anchovies, the radish, green onions, and kelp, add 1 quart of water and bring to a boil. Let the stock simmer for about 20 minutes, then reduce the temperature and simmer on low for another 5 minutes. Pass the stock through a fine-mesh strainer into a second pot and set aside. You will need about 2 cups of the broth.

Peel and mince the garlic and place in another saucepan with the oil, chili flakes, soy sauce, and a little pepper. Cook slowly until the spices get aromatic. Add the seafood and mix well, then pour in the previously measured stock (2 cups) and cook the stew for 2-3 minutes. Clean and roughly chop the mushrooms. Cut the tofu into bite-size pieces. Add the mushrooms and tofu to the stew and stir carefully. Beat the eggs in two small bowls and slide them into the stew.

Bring the stew to a boil and let it simmer for 1–2 minutes. Season to taste with the sesame oil and salt.

To serve

Rinse, trim the root end, and finely chop the green onions. Ladle the stew into deep bowls and garnish with the green onions.

ANDONG

Ginkgo trees and cherry blossoms

Day 4, April 9th. Today is a special day for me because I am meeting Ok-jung. In 2013, she was a cook on my team at the restaurant Spices on Sylt, an island on the North Sea in Germany. Back then, she often expressed surprise over the fact that my Korean dishes tasted if not authentic than close to accurate, without my having ever been to the country. It's been more than four years since we last saw each other; homesickness brought Okjung back to Korea after her time in Germany. Thanks to Facebook, we've stayed in contact and, at the very least, send each other well wishes on our birthdays.

Before this meeting, which I'm very much looking forward to, I will be visiting a historical study site about 6 miles outside Andong: Byeongsan Seowon, which was a Confucian academy during the Joseon Dynasty (1392–1897). The road on the way there is really bumpy, even Ms. Heo is surprised. There are small vegetable fields on the left side of the street. Maybe the academy once provided for itself with food grown on those fields. Once I arrive here, I immediately understand why it would be possible to devote yourself entirely to learning here. The buildings are situated between a river and the imposing backdrop of the small mountains, far outside of any city. The entire place exudes calm and strength. According to Ms. Heo, many famous Korean scholars have studied here.

The division between men and women, Ms. Heo explains, is clearly visible here. The men slept inside the buildings in rooms facing the courtyard. The women had to use a low, side entrance to get into their lounges and bedrooms outside the courtyard, and it was this low entrance that ensured segregation by gender, because generally speaking, only women were small enough to fit through it. It wouldn't have been appropriate anyway for a man to crouch down and make himself smaller than he actually was.

I don't spend enough time in Korea to really experience how far equality has come here in society. Ms. Heo observes that the birth of a son is still more respected than that of a daughter. In principle, the country is really very modern and during my entire trip I never had the feeling that women were not welcome on the street, for example. But of course we were also in a lot of touristy places, which are also definitely more modern.

Emotions and some reflection After the trip to the academy, we continue on to Andong, on the east side of Korea. I finally see Okjung again, and it's a bit like in a movie: We see each other from a distance, run towards each other and hug — an intense, emotional moment on this journey. Since our English vocabularies are limited to small talk, we just laugh a lot and are happy to see each other again. So much has happened in the past four years. I got married. Okjung did too. Like me, she found love at work in the kitchen and is now becoming a mom for the second time. I wish her all the luck in the world! Maybe we'll manage to meet again in Seoul or Jeonju during this trip. In any case, I promised to come back with my husband Christian and show him what I've experienced here.

I get a bit melancholy because only now am I starting to realize that I'm alone here. I'm not truly alone, of course, but I miss having a trusted person that I could share these experiences with. If someone were to ask me at this very moment how I felt here, I wouldn't be able to answer that with one word. Writing my thoughts down really helps me deal with the situation. I'm feeling very grateful that this trip was made possible for me. It's strange to be around people who look like me and yet are somehow different. I ask myself again and again whether the women I meet here could be related to me. The likelihood is very, very small and yet I can't help but wonder. When I was an orphan, and someone found me wandering the streets of Seoul alone, I didn't know many words. Apparently, I kept repeating, "NooNa," which means "sister" in Korean. Does that mean that I wasn't alone? If I wasn't, what became of my sister? Thoughts like that are constantly coursing through my brain. Despite the weight of such questions, I'm still glad to be here, to learn, to try to understand what it's like in my native country. And to be happy that I'm able to go on living as I do, even if it's elsewhere.

Mackerel, chicken and sweet potato glass noodles: We are having lunch at the Andong Jjimdak Market, a traditional market lined with jjimdak (chicken stew) restaurants. It's a nice little square with lots of mini-restaurants, one next to the other. And Andong's specialty is salty mackerel. First, they slit the fish on the belly side. Then they remove the guts, backbone and ribs, and then cut it again on the opposite side, making it possible to spread it flat like a butterfly. Finally, they place it in a salt bath. That's what it looks like, at any rate. To cook it, they place the mackerel on the grill until it's nice and crispy. I'm a little worried that the great crispy color also means that it will be dry. But, happily, it turns out to be super juicy, cooked to the right point, as we cooks say. It's served with bean sprouts, kimchi, pickled pearl onions, green onions, and cucumber.

There's also a second main dish: a huge bowl of chicken and glass noodles with green onions, potatoes, carrots, and cabbage. It's swimming in a stock made of black soybean sauce. The chicken is chopped into bite-size pieces but with its bones. It takes some practice to nibble the meat off the bones. It's unusual but definitely an experience in itself. The glass noodles, which are made from sweet potato starch, are really good. I bet I can get it somewhere at home! (Postscript: I found a dealer who can deliver them to me!)

Ginkgo trees and cherry blossoms. After the market, we go to the famous historical Andong Hahoe Folk Village, which is laid out like a lotus flower, with a 600 year-old tree in the middle. It's customary to write your wishes on a small piece of paper and tie it to the ropes that cordon off the tree. You've probably already noticed from my stories that there are lot of customs here that are supposed to bring luck or make wishes come true. Back home, my husband, Christian, laughs when I tell him about them and says: "With all of the things that they do to bring good luck, the Koreans ought to be the luckiest people in the world." However, I also ask myself, very seriously, whether these elaborate rituals simply encourage a positive attitude? Are the Koreans luckier than we are in Germany? I don't know and my time here is too short to really find out. But I wrote down a wish and tied it to the rope ... I'm not going to tell you what was on the note.

The square with the tree is ringed by about 30 houses, which are surrounded by walls. Inside them, you'll find historical hanok buildings. Unfortunately, none of them are open. Apparently, as Ms. Heo observes, some time ago the careless behavior of some tourists led to the outbreak of fire in the hanoks. You can well imagine the damage a fire would do to a house with roofs covered in dry straw. Because we can't view them up close, we instead walk through the village, only peering at them from the outside. But the Andong Hahoe Folk Village has another incredible attraction: The cherry blossom trees are in full bloom. It's simply amazing – the perfect backdrop for the selfie generation.

An overnight stay the traditional way — and very little sleep. We continue on to the Gurume Hanok Resort. The house I'll be staying in today was originally built in 1740. It used to be located in Seok Jang Ok and housed three generations under one roof. In 2008, they moved it to the Gurume Hanok Resort, where they rebuilt it from the ground up. The entire resort is beautiful. It consists of many small, traditionally constructed houses. We enter an inner courtyard through a large, heavy wooden gate. To the right of the courtyard is an area that's open to the inner courtyard and has a window in the wall to the outside. The windows are made of wooden struts covered with strong paper. The entire interior is minimalist: a small flat table, a vase with wooden branches, white cushions, and that's it. I find it all so incredibly beautiful. It's the spareness that allows the room to hold its own against the rest of the house. From there you move into two rooms, each equipped with a modern bathroom. The first is a small bedroom. I estimate that it's about 8 x 8 feet, with light walls and minimalist furnishings. One wall has a branch attached to two small ropes that serves as a clothesline. That's not a bad idea for even a modern home. On the other side of the wall there's a low sideboard. Two neatly folded sleeping mats lie in one corner. The two mats, placed on top of each other, will be my bed tonight. The pillow that goes with it feels like it's filled with dry rice and reminds me a bit of a cherry stone pillow. As pretty as everything is, throughout my trip so far, sleeping has been less than ideal. I don't sleep so well in strange places. Then there's these hard mats! The ambient floor heating is very pleasant and warm and I fall asleep quickly. But before long, the hard surface (and as guests we even get two sleeping mats) makes my back ache. Oh well! There'll be time for sleep when I'm home again.

天翰五福　地逐三災

The ubiquitous chili paste: Once we've checked in, we head out to Hanok Hotel, where I learn how to make the Korean chili paste that I've come across in practically every restaurant. The basic ingredients are crucial for the chili paste, and they all come from Andong: chili powder; fermented black soybeans (meju) that has been dried and ground into a powder; barley malt powder (yeotgireum); and rice juice for which apple juice is an acceptable substitute. That's what I opt for. When I make it, I start by mixing the light barley malt with the apple juice. I then add the precisely weighed chili powder, a little salt, and finally the soybean powder. It tastes pretty good, but it's still missing a bit of depth. I pour my homemade paste into a glass jar that I can take home. Apparently, you should first store it at room temperature so that the paste can still ferment. Then later, once it's reached the ideal state, you should store it in a cool place. If a layer of mold forms, it's not that big of a deal; you can simply scrape it off. Aha! We'll see how it goes. I still get to try a chili paste that's already been refined with garlic and fermented. Wow! It really has "oomph" and tastes delicious.

Every region in Korea has its own recipe for chili paste. And since it's also a basic ingredient in the preparation of kimchi, the kimchi tastes different in each region. I'll have to think about a dish with chili paste for the menu at Yoso. Before we say goodbye, our Korean cooking teacher really wants to take a selfie with me. Ms. Heo had told her about me, and now she's really excited. I'm happy to do it.

Dinner Time – served with love: We go to dinner in a traditional Korean restau- rant. Low tables and cush- ions, no decorations, not even a flower on the table. But that's almost always the case here. There's cut- lery and sometimes a place mat, but nothing else. They bring out a chair without legs for the Europeans so that we can lean on it. The menu is in Korean. Luck- ily, Ms. Heo is there and orders for me. And for the first time we have to wait for the food. Up to now whenever we've ordered it feels like mere seconds before they've brought the first side dishes (banchan) to the table. At this particular restaurant, when the bowls arrive, I'm surprised at how nicely they'e presented. There's a real love for detail behind it, and that makes my cook's heart beat a little faster. There are at least three different salads that have to be marinated

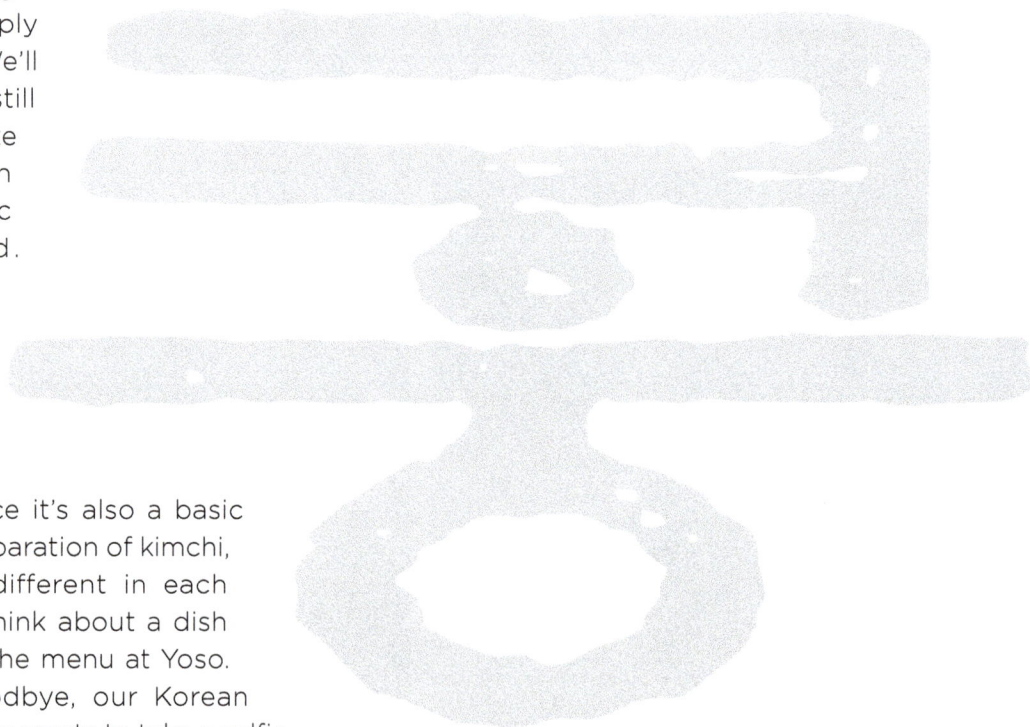

with dressing "à la minute." Otherwise, they'd collapse and get mushy.

Ms. Heo orders bibimbap with raw beef and beef bulgogi for us. I'm eager to try the beef bulgogi, since we have it on the menu at Yoso, but served with mackerel. The bulgogi from Fugo in Busan was completely different from the bulgogi here. This time the taste of the marinade is very close to the bulgogi at Yoso. The beef is cut into very thin strips and marinated. It's grilled and served with various vegetables. The beef tartare is not cut into cubes like we do in Germany; it's cut into thin strips and dressed with roasted sesame oil, fresh green chili peppers, white sesame seeds, and green onions. It's delicious. I should write it down as an idea for the new menu. I'm impressed with the meal and find that, compared to our other culinary experiences so far, it features a wider variety of flavors that you can taste and even anticipate by its appearance. The way it's been arranged with such loving detail, also distinguishes it from the other places we've visited so far. That makes it all the more surprising when Ms. Heo says that this restaurant is not more expensive. The seafood restaurant in the Jagalchi Market in Busan was the most expensive one so far, and she doesn't find the food better here than elsewhere. It's probably my Western tastes. Some of the dishes in this place remind me of familiar tastes, but some of the flavors are completely new to me. In most of the restaurants that we've visited so far, a lot of the dishes have been seasoned with red chili sauce. At this place, though, the chef brought in some sweetness now and again. They serve, for instance, a chicken salad with a honey-mustard dressing, which, when I think about it, is a more Western way to prepare it. So, in the end, I guess Ms. Heo is right after all; it's not better, but it's definitely "more Western" here. Any way you look at, it's very good.

Different countries, different cooking and eating customs: I think I now understand what the chef on "Korea Live" meant when he said that my cuisine was not authentic, but that I could make a lot of money with it in Korea. Here, they serve ingredients individually, then you put the dish together yourself. Like most other chefs in Europe, I serve plated meals. Because the food all comes on one plate, I use different components or combine textures and certain elements with one another. I make it easy for the guest because, essentially, I tell them, "Here's your plate. Enjoy." So even if I use Korean flavors and tastes, it will never be authentic. Since this way of serving is something special in Korea, it could easily become a huge hit. However, I'm not planning to emigrate, so I'll have to let someone else do it. But I still visit a few Michelin-starred restaurants whose chefs are at least as good at preparing plated dishes as their colleagues in Germany.

There's one thing I really like about Korean food culture; they treat dining as a shared experience, a feeling reinforced by the fact that everyone helps themselves from the bowls in the middle. I try to bring a bit of this back home to Germany. On my latest menu, "My trip to Korea in Seven Courses," I offer an entree with three different bowls and a main plate. The customers love it; for them, it's a unique way to dine, something special.

As we're about to leave the restaurant, I notice some very large transparent plastic containers that are filled with about 4 to 6 gallons of dark liquid. I ask Ms. Heo if she wouldn't mind asking the restaurant what it is. One of the servers replies, "It's our homemade dressing." Seconds later, a man rushes up to us. As it turns out, he's the assistant chef. He proudly explains that they bottle their own fruit in the containers for the dressing. He then motions for me to follow him. We walk away from the guest area and come to a staircase. There are even more of these large containers on the steps. I count at least 20 as we go down the stairs. A wide variety of different kinds of food have been placed in them and are fermenting. I'm thrilled. I'd hoped to get a l ook behind the scenes like this. When Ms. Heo tells the cook that I'm a Michelin-starred chef from Germany, he's impressed and we bow to each other.

Day 5, April 10th. From Andong to Seoul. This morning I again enjoy a very traditional Korean breakfast. Instead of bread and jam, it includes rice, kimchi, soup, and all sorts of other things such as boiled beef, two boiled quail eggs in a black soybean sauce, and lightly salted, deep-fried nori leaves to wrap the rice in. I find this type of breakfast amazing.

Normally, it's not polite to watch other people eat, but this morning I can't help but watch how the other people at the restaurant eat their meal. There's a mother sitting at one of the low tables with her children, who are eating breakfast differently than the adults I've observed so far: they are tearing up the nori sheets and putting them in the rice bowl with the vegetables, mixing everything together, and then eating them with a spoon. Korean breakfast cereal? A mere observation. I soak up all the impressions around me. The other guests quickly eat everything separately with the chopsticks. Every now and then they slurp some soup. I don't see anyone reading newspapers, as you would in just about any hotel in Europe. Everyone is concentrating on their food, something of which I heartily approve. There's only one thing missing: coffee. In its place, they serve a very spicy tea (I can taste cinnamon and ginger). It tastes good, but after another night on the hard floor I could still really use the coffee. The bright sun quickly chases away my fatigue and I'm ready to start the day. The building exudes a calm, almost meditative atmosphere. It's probably exactly what you imagine when you think of traditional Korean hanok buildings. It's the perfect place for writing. When I arrived here yesterday, I'd hoped that today the sun would be shining and that I could find a nice place to continue writing in my journal. How lucky then that I find a sort of pavilion that's surrounded by a tiny stream. Maybe in Korea wishes really do come true. The setting is beautiful. In every direction I look, there's an incredible backdrop. I feel so good that I'm reluctant to leave. In a place like this, writing comes easily.

I think about what's ahead in the next few days. I've already learned a lot about the history and traditions of Korea. Later today we'll be traveling to Seoul, the capital. I'm supposed to stay there for five days. There are 26 million people living in the larger metropolitan area of Seoul, and almost 42,000 inhabitants per square mile in Seoul itself. I'm curious how I'll get my bearings there. After all, I grew up in the countryside and later lived on the tranquil island of Sylt for three years. A few years ago, I visited Bangkok. I found it a real challenge. The hustle and bustle, the crowds and many tuk tuks (motorized rickshaws)! I hope my first impression of Seoul isn't too disappointing and that things are less chaotic there.

We're traveling by train again. Just as I was on my previous train ride, I'm delighted with how comfortable the seats are and by how friendly the staff is. The free WiFi is great!

Seoul, here I come!

Godeungeo-gui
Grilled Mackerel

고등어조림

Serves 4 | Prep time: **50 minutes** | Marinating time: **2 hours**

For the godeungeo-gui
2 mackerel
2 tablespoons coarse sea
salt
2 tablespoons neutral
  vegetable oil

To serve
Various kimchi varieties
Sprouts

Godeungeo-gui
Clean the mackerel inside and out and rinse it under cold running water. Separate the head and fins, if desired. Cut the fish lengthwise on the belly side and unfold both halves. Cut a few cross sections into the fillets up to the bones. Season the fillets with the salt and cover with cling film. Let the mackerel rest in the refrigerator for about 2 hours, then carefully pat the fillets dry.

Heat the oil over medium heat in a grill pan. Grill the mackerel, skin side down, for 2-3 minutes, then turn and grill the meat side for 2-3 minutes longer.

To serve
Serve the grilled mackerel on a platter and place a selection of side dishes in separate bowls.

Jjimdak
Braised Chicken with Noodles and Vegetables

닭찜

Serves 4 | Prep time: **70 minutes** | Marinating time: **20 minutes**

For the Jjimdak
1 whole chicken
(approx. 2 lb / 1 kg)
4 tablespoons mirin (rice wine)
1 tablespoon salt
Freshly ground black pepper
2 waxy potatoes
2 large carrots
1 large onion
1/4 head of Chinese cabbage
1 bunch green onions
3 shiitake mushrooms (as desired)
2-3 dried red chili peppers
6 tablespoons soy sauce
3 tablespoons sugar
2 cloves garlic, peeled and finely chopped
4 tablespoons neutral vegetable oil
¼ cup (30 g) grated ginger
4 oz (120 g) dried glass noodles
1 tablespoon white sesame seeds

Jjimdak

Rinse the chicken and pat dry. Cut the chicken into small pieces using poultry shears and a knife and place the pieces in a large bowl. Mix half of the rice wine (2 tablespoons) with the salt and a pinch of pepper. Pour the marinade over the chicken pieces and mix everything well. Cover and let the chicken rest for about 20 minutes.

Peel the potatoes and carrots and cut them into small pieces. Peel the onion and cut into thin wedges. Rinse the Chinese cabbage, green onions, and mushrooms and cut into bite-size pieces. Remove the seeds from the chili peppers and finely chop.

For the seasoning sauce, combine the soy sauce, sugar, remaining rice wine (2 tablespoons) and garlic in a bowl.

Heat the oil in a large skillet over medium heat. Slowly cook the ginger and chili peppers until fragrant. Add chicken, skin side down, and pan fry for 3-5 minutes until they are golden brown. Flip chicken and cook 3-5 minutes more. Remove chicken from pan and let drain on a plate lined with paper towels.

Put the chicken, chopped potatoes, carrots, and onion wedges in a large saucepan and mix in the seasoning sauce. Pour about 3 cups of water over the chicken so that it is completely covered with liquid. Bring the liquid to a boil and let the contents of the pot simmer for about 20 minutes.

In the meantime, soak the glass noodles in cold water according to the instructions on the package. Drain the noodles in a colander and add to the pot with the chicken. Add the green onions, Chinese cabbage, and (if used) the mushrooms. Let everything simmer for another 10 minutes. Toast the sesame seeds in a non-stick pan, without oil, then stir in at the end.

To serve
Arrange the chicken, noodles, and vegetables on deep plates and serve.

Bibimbap
Rice with vegetable and beef

비빔밥

Serves 4 | Prep time: 45 minutes | Marinating time: 60 minutes

For the bibimbap

4 green onions
1 clove of garlic
2 tablespoons soy sauce, a
  little more for the spinach
1 tablespoon sugar
1 tablespoon sesame oil
2 tablespoons toasted
  sesame oil
2/3 lb (300 g) beef
  shoulder, cut in thin strips
10 cups (300 g) fresh
  spinach
2 carrots
1 ½ cups (200 g) daikon
  radish
2 cups (150 g) mung bean
  sprouts
Salt
1 tablespoon neutral
  vegetable oil
1 teaspoon white sesame
  seeds
1 red chili pepper
1 green chili pepper
Freshly ground black
  pepper

To serve

3 cups (1 kg) cooked rice
Toasted sesame oil
Gochujang (spicy Korean
  chili paste)

Bibimbap

Rinse, trim the root end, and finely chop the green onions. Peel and mince the garlic. In a large bowl, combine the soy sauce, sugar, sesame oil, 1 tablespoon toasted sesame oil, garlic, and green onions. Add beef, making sure the beef is completely covered with the marinade. Cover the bowl with a lid and refrigerate for 1 hour.

Clean, trim, and drain the spinach. Peel the carrots and radish and cut into very fine strips. Clean and drain the bean sprouts. Heat a large saucepan with salted water and blanch the vegetables separately, one after the other: the carrots and radish each for 1 minute and the mung bean sprouts for 30 seconds, draining well after removing from hot water. Lightly salt the carrots. Mix the bean sprouts with 1 teaspoon toasted sesame oil.

Heat the vegetable oil in the same pan over medium heat. Add spinach and cook until it is slightly wilted. Remove spinach from pan and drain well. In a medium bowl, mix the wilted spinach with ½ teaspoon of toasted sesame oil and some soy sauce.

Toast the sesame seeds in a non-stick pan, without oil. Rinse and core the chili peppers and cut into thin rings. Heat remaining vegetable oil in a pan until smoking hot. Add beef and sear both sides until desired doneness. For medium rare, about 1 minute each side. Season to taste with pepper before serving.

To serve

Arrange the different vegetables in a circle in deep bowls and arrange the beef in the middle. Garnish with the sesame seeds and pepper rings. Serve with the rice, sesame oil, and gochujang.

Bulgogi
Bulgogi

불고기

Serves 4 | Prep time: **45 minutes** | Marinating time: **30 minutes**

For the bulgogi
2 bunches green onions
2 cloves garlic
1 medium (150 g) Asian
  pears
3 tablespoons white sesame
  seeds
7 tablespoons soy sauce
4 tablespoons sugar
1 tablespoon freshly grated
  ginger
2 tablespoons toasted
  sesame oil
1/2 teaspoon freshly ground
black pepper
2 tablespoons cheongju
  (clear, refined Korean rice
  wine)
1 ¾ lb (800 g) beef
  tenderloin
1 large onion
3 ½ oz (100 g) shiitake
  mushrooms
2 tablespoons neutral
  vegetable oil

Bulgogi
Rinse, trim the root end, and finely chop green onions for the marinade, setting aside half for garnish. Peel and finely chop the garlic. Peel and core the pear and finely grate the flesh. Toast the sesame seeds in a pan, without oil.

In a large bowl, mix the green onion, garlic, and grated pear puree, and 2 tablespoons of the toasted sesame seeds with the soy sauce, sugar, ginger, sesame oil, pepper, and rice wine.

Trim excess skin from the beef, then cut into thin, bite-size slices against the grain. Put the meat slices in the bowl with the marinade and stir, making sure that the beef is completely covered with the marinade. Cover and let the beef marinate in the refrigerator for at least 30 minutes and up to 2 hours.

Peel the onion and cut into thin wedges. Clean and finely dice the mushrooms. Take the meat out of the refrigerator and mix in the onions and mushrooms. Heat the oil in the pan over high heat. Stir fry the meat and vegetables in batches until charred and cooked through, about 6-8 minutes. While you stir fry the remaining portions, keep the already cooked bulgogi warm in a separate pan with some of the sauce from the main pan. (The meat can also be cooked in a grill pan or over a charcoal grill.)

To serve
Arrange the bulgogi on preheated plates and garnish with the remaining toasted sesame seeds (1 tablespoon!) and the finely chopped green onion.

TIP

Other vegetables, like chopped carrots, can be added to bulgogi. Kimchi makes for a good side dish. For more spice, before serving, sprinkle some fresh chili pepper rings over it.

Dubu Jorim
Braised Tofu in Soy Sauce

두부조림

Serves 4 | Prep time: **30 minutes** | Marinating time: **60 minutes**

For the dubu jorim
1 lb (500 g) firm tofu
1 tablespoon white sesame
    seeds
1 onion
1 clove of garlic
1 bunch green onions
1 teaspoon toasted sesame
    oil
1 tablespoon soy sauce
1 teaspoon salt
1 teaspoon sugar
1 tablespoon gochujang
    (spicy Korean chili paste)
1 tablespoon gochugaru
    (Korean chili flakes)
3 tablespoons neutral
    vegetable oil

To serve
1 bunch chrysanthemum
    greens

Dubu jorim
Drain the tofu and wrap it in a cloth. Place this packet in a fine-mesh strainer and weigh it down lightly so that any excess liquid can drain off. (The block of tofu should keep its shape.)

Toast the sesame seeds in a non-stick pan, without oil, allow to cool and grind into a powder with a mortar and pestle.

Mince the garlic. Rinse, trim the root end, and finely dice the green onions.

In a medium bowl, combine the ground toasted sesame seeds, the onion, garlic, and green onion as well as the sesame oil, soy sauce, salt, sugar, gochujang, and gochugaru to create a spicy sauce and set aside. If necessary, stir in some water.

Cut the tofu into 1-inch cubes. Heat the oil in a pan over medium-high heat. Working in batches, add the tofu pieces in a single layer and fry until golden brown on all sides. In a saucepan, warm spicy sauce over medium heat. Add the fried tofu and gently stir until tofu is completely covered with the sauce.

To serve
Arrange the fried tofu with the spicy sauce on plates and garnish with the chrysanthemum greens.

SEOUL

Paradise for lovers of fish and Korean cuisine

Day 5, April 10th. Arrival with a bit of trouble. Thanks to the travel agency's plans and Kore's good infrastructure, I've been getting around pretty well. Today it's a little more challenging. When I arrive at the train station in Seoul, first I have to find the right exit for the taxis. After a few wrong turns, I find myself standing outside on the street. I stop a taxi, show the driver the name of the hotel, which my travel app has kindly translated into Korean — and he waves me off, leaving me there with my luggage. Was he unable to read the name? Had the app translated it incorrectly or did he not know the hotel? I'm a bit lost. I try another taxi and fail. Brash locals are faster than I am. What a contrast to the last two days in the quiet, relaxed Gurume Hanok Resort.

Fortunately, a Korean woman who speaks English is watching me. She asks if she can help. I'm so relieved. Three taxis drive past her and she scolds them loudly. Then it occurs to me: Trying to catch a cab here is an adventure. When she finally manages to stop a taxi, the driver points out that we're on the wrong side of the street. Aha! To get to the correct side, we have to cross what feels like ten lanes, three of which are for buses. When we're finally on the right side, a taxi immediately stops. I quickly put my suitcases in the taxi – mine has to be put on the passenger seat, because most taxis in Korea run on gas and the gas container is in the trunk and takes up a lot of space. Off we go to the hotel. The aggressive way the driver navigates traffic, makes me so nervous that my only thought is: I hope we arrive safely at the hotel. But amidst the winding streets, the driver can't find the hotel right away and asks me for its phone number. I have it written on a piece of paper. But he can't read it because he isn't wearing his glasses. Our communication breaks down even further and the driver starts getting pretty loud at this point. Right about now, I'm feeling really glad that I've got my photographer with me. But before things get too crazy, the driver somehow figures out where the hotel is, and we finally arrive. The hotel is friendly and everything comes off without a hitch, and I can settle into my room for the next five days.

First search for "Seoul Food." Maybe it's because of my job, but I've barely been in my room and have already started wondering where I could go to dinner tonight. That's impossible to plan for, though, because the new guide hasn't even arrived yet. However, on the taxi ride to the hotel, I noticed a few small alleys nearby with illuminated signs suggesting that they are restaurants. I decide to go explore them. First, I take a look at a few of the places from the outside. Then I choose one that offers Korean BBQ. I've heard so much about it. I want to try it myself finally. Like most small restaurants, this one is really a sort of nicely outfitted, street food stand with a menu hanging out front; it's filled with Koreans only. Men of different ages occupy two tables. There's a young couple seated at another table. I'm situated at a table that is somewhat in the middle. Dining like this is what I'm finding so exciting about this trip; I'm experiencing how the locals really eat, how they celebrate food, and how uncomplicated it all is. Sometimes you get the impression that people are always eating in Korea. That's probably because you see a lot of people eating out. People like to eat with friends here. Most do that in restaurants, because apartments in Seoul are not particularly large, given the 25 million people who live here.

My Korean BBQ is heavenly! Fortunately, the menu in "my" restaurant is also written in English. So I order beef and pork belly. I've been looking forward to the pork belly for days. I got to know and love our Korean sushi chef Mijum years ago at the restaurant Spices. After the friendly, older server took my order, she came back a short time later with different bowls: kimchi, pickled and thinly sliced daikon, lettuce leaves, perilla leaves, ssamjang consisting of red chili pepper paste, toasted sesame oil, toasted sesame seeds, rice syrup, and chopped garlic. Once she has turned on the table grill, she puts the pork belly and beef slices and a couple of garlic slices on the grill. As soon as the first slices of grilled meat are finished, she cuts the pork belly into bite-size pieces with scissors and shows me how to eat them. She looks after me a bit like a mom. I'm pretty sure she only does that with people who have never eaten Korean BBQ before. She probably took one glance at me and knew that I had never tried it.

The first thing I do is take a leaf of lettuce, put a piece of meat on it and coat the whole thing with a little ssamjang. Then I add a slice of garlic, some lettuce cut into small pieces, topped with a spicy dressing, and finally I roll up the leaf and take a bite. Delicious! Now I understand why so many people rave about Korean BBQ. I love it too! It may be a fairly simple meal, but it's more about the experience of eating this way. Rolling the various ingredients in the leaves is fun. The taste is an incredible mixture of smoky flavors, spice from the ssamjang paste, balanced against the slight acidity of the dressed lettuce leaves. The addition of vegetables adds a fresh, crunchy texture. You could get addicted to eating like this.

You can see and hear just how much the guests are enjoying their meal, and how easy it can be to inspire such an atmosphere. Even Michelin-starred chefs want our guests to have fun while eating, and they pull that off here with a piece of grilled meat, a lettuce leaf, and a slice of garlic. Brilliant! My wheels start turning: How can I incorporate this experience into a dish at Yoso? Another small addendum: Yoso now has pork belly BBQ with perilla leaves, which guests can wrap up in lettuce leaves themselves if they want to.

Day 6, April 11th. Day for eating. There's no breakfast in the hotel, which turns out to be a blessing considering the many food stops that I'll be making today. My new guide is Jain and we hit if off right away. This might have something to do with the fact that she's also worked as a chef.

From the start, I'm grateful to Jain, and even more so in hindsight. Over the course of our days together, she shared a lot of private things about her life. She had an incredible impact on my trip. She helped me understand even better what life in Korea is really like. No matter how many guidebooks you read, ultimately, it's the people and their personal stories that bring a country closer to you. Jain, who is in her late twenties, worked abroad for a number of years but is now back with her family outside of Seoul. Several days a week she spends two hours in the morning and two hours in the evening commuting to and from the capital on the train. I won't recount everything we talked about because that's her story. I will share, however, that I'm touched that she confided that one of her many siblings was given up for adoption because the family didn't have a lot of money. Thank you, Jain, for your trust in telling me so much and for showing me your Korea.

In "hot meal in the morning heaven." Our first destination today is Namdaemun Market. If you're like me and prefer to eat soup or fried noodles rather than toast with jam for breakfast, you'll find a little paradise here. I feel like I'm in "hot-meal-in-the-morning heaven." First, I try the kimbap, which looks a lot like Japanese sushi rolls. However, the rice is seasoned with salt and sesame oil, and the kimbap rolls don't contain raw fish but are filled with seasoned vegetables and steamed egg. The kimbap that they serve for breakfast are smaller, similar in size to maki rolls. There are also large kimbap rolls that you have to cut into thin slices to even fit them in your mouth. The next dish warms my heart: kimchi noodle soup with tofu and cabbage – it feels kind of homey, even if I didn't grow up with it. They also serve bibimbap, which I am already familiar with, for breakfast here. But thanks to Jain, I finally learn how to eat the dish. You have to mix and stir the ingredients really well; that's the only way to do it. Ms. Heo had already told me that I had to mix it all up, but I was far too timid. As the last breakfast meal choice for today, I try the guksu ("knife cut noodle soup"). It's a soup into which they cut freshly made noodles and then let them cook in the broth. Such a fantastic breakfast! I'm ready to discover the market.

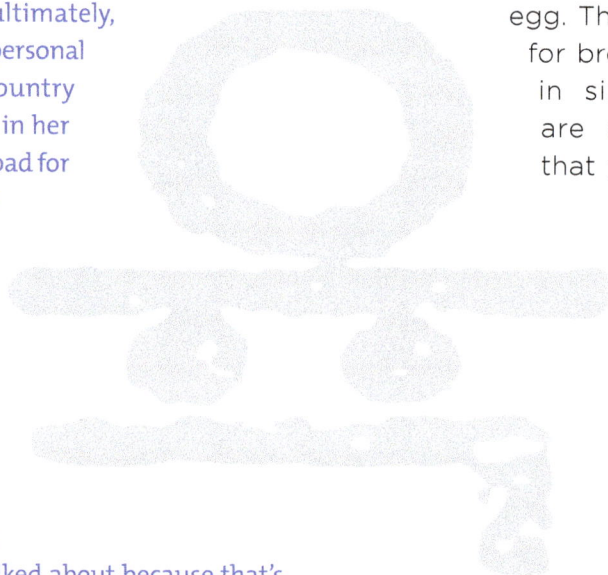

In Korea they have a saying, "If you can't find it in Namdaemun Market, you won't find anywhere." And that's truly how it looks. Everything is colorful, and there's a lot of everything. Still, I don't see anything that I absolutely have to have. In the middle of the market there's also a six-story department store. There's one floor devoted to dishes and household utensils, which speaks to my inner chef. It's a good thing that I have only a small baggage allowance and therefore have to be satisfied with a baking mold and two mats for steam baskets. Just looking is a lot of fun. The fragrance emanating from the next floor reveals what you'll find there: flowers! I've never seen so many in one room!

Culture walk: We resist the urge to indulge in a shopping spree. We continue to Gyeongbokgung Palace — a famous tourist attraction, guarded by strict guards who have to stand for two hours without moving. Their glued-on beards give them away as actors. There's a ceremonious changing of the guard, just like in front of Buckingham Palace in London. Unlike there, though, here it's merely a big show for visitors. But I am a visitor too! So, I also have to have my picture taken. The mixture of traditional and the modern in Korea becomes very clear here. If you look in one direction, you see the palace entrance with the mountains in the background, and if you turn in the complete opposite direction, you see modern skyscrapers. Between the towers, stand two famous sculptures, one of which appears on one of the Korean banknotes.

We walk from the palace towards Bukchon Hanok Village. Though it's a major tourist attraction in the heart of the city, that is not how it started out. During the Joseon Dynasty, the aristocracy lived here, close to the palace. Their former homes, traditional hanok houses, are now protected as part of a historical preservation project. Here you can find small restaurants, art galleries, and workshops where you can learn traditional crafts. The clocks seem to tick more slowly here. Their historical significance aside, the houses provide a wonderful backdrop for souvenir pictures: Many tourists rent traditional Korean robes and pose for friends who take photos or they take selfies. It's not only Korean tourists posing in traditional garb; many of them come from China. I wouldn't have realized that, had Jain not pointed it out

A peaceful teatime. After we've taken a few photos, we stop at a teahouse. It's such a place of calm, which is wonderful after the hustle and bustle of the city! We sit on cushions on the ground with a low table in front of us. I order a "Mulberry Leaves Tea."

The server places a small tray with the tea utensils in front of me, and Jain shows me how to make the tea. My miniature teapot is filled with mulberry leaves. I pour hot water into the teapot from a thermos flask, let everything steep for 30 seconds and then pour the tea through a sieve into my tea mug. Jain explains that you can infuse the leaves three times in the pot but that the third infusion tastes best. A small plate of Korean pastries, such as deep-fried rice cakes, sesame, walnut, and mixed-nut cookies, is served with the tea. We sit back and enjoy the tea and the peace and quiet.

Chicken in restaurant frequented by celebrities – Kimchi in the cooking school.

The short break in the tea house did us some good, because it's already time for lunch. We'll be eating in a restaurant that's frequented by Korean celebrities, as the numerous pictures in the entrance area attest. The specialty here is samgyetang (ginseng chicken soup) with a whole young chicken. The chicken is stuffed with rice and cooked in a broth with green onions and ginseng and then served in a cast iron pot. The usual bowls with kimchi, tofu, and daikon are of course also available. The soup is good, but to be honest I don't quite understand the hype that Jain says people in Seoul make about this restaurant. But that's often the way it is with businesses frequented by celebrities.

Next on the agenda is a cooking school. It's owned by O'ngo Food, the company that organized my trip and is run by Jain's boss. Today I'm learning how to make kimchi and bulgogi from one of O'ngo's chefs, Jia Choi. At Yoso, I also have a dish with kimchi on the menu. However, mine is only marinated, not fermented. And the difference is huge when I compare it with this one here in Korea. Kimchi, as I've discovered during this trip, can be prepared a variety of ways; there is no one authentic recipe. It's been served with almost every meal, at least twice a day. In fact, there are up to 170 different varieties. Every region in Korea has its own way of preparing it (and chili pepper paste too) that relies on regional ingredients. Despite their many differences, they nonetheless all share the same, unmistakable smell produced by the fermentation process. Kimchi can change its taste from one day to the next. Tomorrow you can detect a different nuance than you might today. It's a living product, which keeps it unpredictable and exciting.

Delicious bulgogi – I'm gradually getting full!

Bulgogi is a classic Korean dish that means "fire meat." Because of my "bulgogi style" dish at Yoso, I'm again extremely curious to see how well I approximate the real thing, and in fact the marinade that we make here at Jia Choi's school is actually very close to my "mackerel bulgogi style." The basic ingredients are soy sauce, sugar, sesame oil, lots of garlic, and finely grated fresh pears (which I replace with pear juice).

In Korea, they often mix freshly grated pears with meat marinades, because an enzyme in the pear breaks up the meat structure, making it softer and juicier when cooked. Kiwi and pineapple can also be used instead of pears, but since their enzymes each have a slightly different effect on the meat, you have to adjust the proportions when marinating. Jia Choi explains that the marinated meat should be left in the refrigerator overnight, if possible, so that the marinade is absorbed well. Some vegetable oil is then heated in a pan and the beef is seared in it. It's garnished with green onions and sesame seeds. The finished bulgogi can then be wrapped in lettuce or perilla leaves and enjoyed immediately. This gives me a few ideas of how I could serve a dish like this at Yoso.

Jia Choi fries us a crispy kimchi pancake with some seafood as a side dish. The pancake consists only of water, flour, gochujang, and kimchi. She fries it until golden brown and crispy, the way she likes it best. It's a bit unusual but tastes delicious. I wish I were hungrier because everything here tastes so good. But because I've already tried and eaten so much today, I simply can't take another bite. Plus, I need a little time to digest before tonight, when I'm going on a food tour.

"Food tour de force" with a great team The food tour starts around 6 p.m. My guide is Kay, a young Korean. Four different places where you can try traditional Korean dishes and drinks are on the itinerary. Besides me, our group consists of five other foodies who want to learn about Korean food: Two Korean women who, if I've understood correctly, are attending a culinary school; two girls from Taiwan who are on vacation in Seoul; and Vijay, who was born in India but now lives with his family in California and wanted to complement a business trip with this tour. We hit it off right away and talk about (what else?) food with a mixture of English and gestures.

Tour stop 1: Korean outdoor BBQ. Large metal barrels are set up in front of the restaurant and serve as a table and/or table grill. All of the seats are occupied; it's lively, as usual. There's a nice buzz from being right in the middle of the action. You can compare the atmosphere a bit with a crowded German beer garden during a festival. It's loud and amusing —without even a festival going on. It's simply everyday life, which makes it even nicer. First things first, Kay orders a "special" drink for us: gojingamrae, which translates as "sweet after bitter." This is my first time experiencing a drink like this. They fill a glass with about 6 oz of cola, then add a shot of soju, followed by a shot of beer. I'm shaking a little inside, because I don't like the taste of beer, but I'm in for a penny, in for a pound, so we toast each other in Korean: "geonbae!" It isn't going to be the last "geonbae" tonight. It's also a fun way to get to know each other and introduce people of different nationalities to each other.

I always say that "food connects people and makes them happy." Tonight proves it. The meal brought us together and it's evident that we're all feeling pretty good. I bet you're wondering: How did the gojingamrae taste? I would say "okay." It wasn't half as bad as I feared it might be because the last thing that hits my taste buds is the cola. I can imagine that a few more rounds of gojingamrae would inspire our group to have an even better time than we're already having.

But now back to the meal, in this case an outdoor version of Korean BBQ. Since I already had BBQ on my first evening in Seoul (was it just yesterday?), I'm practically a skilled BBQ eater today and, know what to expect, in theory at least. I'm curious how it will taste here. Vijay explains that he's had Korean BBQ in California. But when the first ingredients are placed on the table, he's taken aback and says that things look very different at home. We all have to laugh. We have a lot of fun together, and because there are many other groups of locals sitting around us and enjoying everything loudly, we feel like we're right at the center of Korean life.

Sharing a meal is twice as fun! Raw pork and beef slices are brought to the table and placed on the grill. The person sitting closest to the grill is given the tongs and is the grill master for the night. In addition to meat, you can also grill garlic or fresh green peppers. Tonight, there's a new ingredient added to the grill: king oyster mushrooms. And, of course, there's kimchi. Each guest receives a bowl filled with onion slices and green onions in a marinade made from soy sauce, rice syrup, and rice vinegar. As always, all the other bowls are put on the table for everyone to share. This encourages communication to take place naturally, something that really appeals to me. People who don't know each other get into conversation a lot faster than if everyone were sitting in front of their own plate. To season the grilled meat, there's a bowl with fermented soybean powder, salt, and roasted and ground perilla seeds. They cut the meat into bite-size pieces table side as well. Kay shows us how to hold the lettuce leaves in your hand and, then one after the other, lay the various ingredients on top of each another, roll them up, and enjoy. I'm now definitely a fan of Korean BBQ. The others apparently are too, because the mountains of meat have disppeared before we move on to the next stop on the tour.

Tour stop 2: Seafood Toppoki. I probably wouldn't have visited the next restaurant without Kay, because of its truly unassuming appearance, but that's what a food tour is for, introducing you to places you wouldn't have discovered otherwise. Two gas stoves are set up in front of us, with two large pans on them. One of them is filled with seafood, strips of fish cake, rice cake rolls, which I already tried during my first meal in Busan, a red stock, and thin noodles. The noodles look undercooked, and the seafood is obviously raw. After a few minutes, I get the point behind it: They finish cooking the dish, seafood toppoki at the table, by allowing it to simmer for a bit longer. It tastes spicy, a little fishy, aromatic, and simply good. The thin noodles, which remind me of spaghetti, soak up the stock perfectly. There's a serious risk that I may develop an addiction to yet another Korean dish. That wasn't going to happen today, though, as I ate as much BBQ as I could and after just sampling a portion of the toppoki I cannot eat anymore. Seafood toppoki is really popular in Korea, but somehow it wasn't on my "What do I have to eat when I'm in Korea" list. So I'm really grateful for the chance to try it.

We still have the second pot, the contents of which are brought to a boil on the gas stove. The stock is not as spicy, and in addition to the slices of fish cake and meat, there are also dumplings with some kind of meat filling in them. I can't pinpoint the exact composition of this filling, but it's very good. Kay orders us two bottles of plum wine. I've had plum wine before, and I like it better than gojingamrae. I treat myself to a second small glass and feel a bit like I'm in heaven. I'm feeling good, and am happy that I can share this evening with the others.

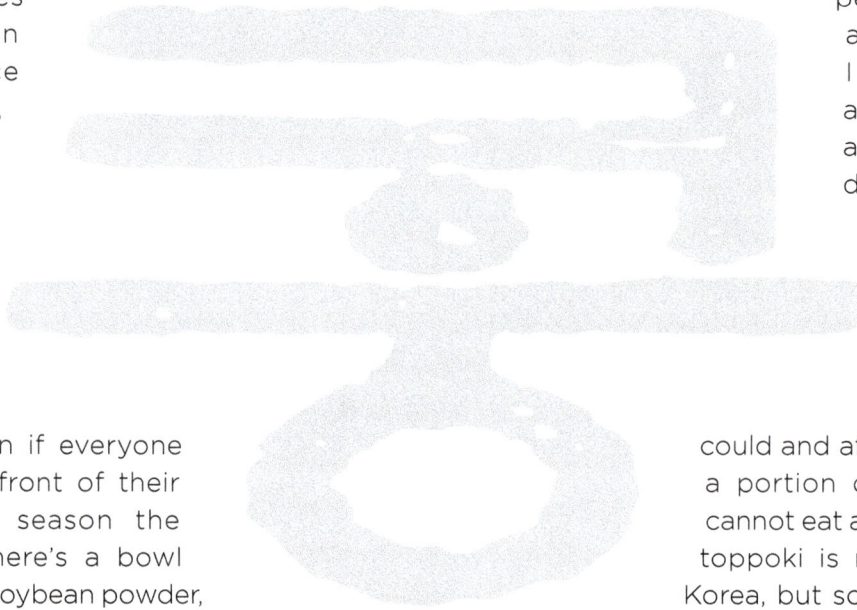

Tour stop 3: A Korean pub. The next stop on our food tour leads us to a kind of Korean pub (my interpretation), which, like many places here, is very full. There are, as there were elsewhere, a few pictures of Korean celebrities hanging in the entryway. I think it's like a pub because the interior is mostly made of dark wood (no plastic chairs and wax tablecloths, which I've gotten used to by now). Beer is served in a large pitcher, and there are snacks in two large bowls to nibble on: natural chicken and chicken in a red, spicy-looking marinade. Plus, there's a cast iron pan in which a chicken in garlic marinade is still sizzling. When I say "garlic marinade" I mean *garlic!* You should only eat this marinade if you will be spending the night alone or with someone who also ate it. Garlic issues aside, I'm getting really full, but it's hard to stop eating this dish!

Koreans love picnics, Kay shares apropos of nothing. It's part of Korean culture to meet up with friends and family for big picnics on the Han River or in Korea's other great parks, just as soon as the weather permits. You can bring your own food and drinks or have it delivered to you from so-called "chicken and beer restaurants." You tell them where to meet you, and the food is delivered by moped. The driver calls as soon as he's at the meeting point and asks the customer to stand up and wave. It's an efficient way for the customer and delivery person to find each other, and to start the picnic once it's arrived. In fact, two days later we see several larger groups who have made themselves comfortable outside on blankets. It's April, so still rather cool, but they're having a great time and enjoying life. In any case, I think that when it comes to eating at least, Koreans seem a lot more joyful and happier than many Germans do.

I'm not the only one who's pretty full; the others are slowly weakening too — only Vijay bravely continues to eat. However, he also came straight to the food tour after a long flight, so it's no wonder that he's so hungry. Since I've been eating from morning to night here, I haven't been hungry since I arrived. Amazingly, I don't feel bloated either; on the contrary, I can tell how healthy the food is, with very little fat or side dishes that are too filling. Well, apart from the rice cakes and pancakes.

Tour stop 4: A tea house with a surprisingly good dessert. Kay leaves it up to us to decide whether we want to walk through the night market as the last stop or visit a tea house that also serves dessert. The female majority favors dessert. Fortunately for me, it's not as sweet as I'd feared it might be. After trying a small piece, I can honestly say that I will never grow to love the universally popular rice cake, which is wrapped in batter and baked. The second dessert is more to my taste, and although I'm really full, I have a little something more: a dessert that comes in a single large bowl with a green "lid" (and looks like a soufflé). It's frozen granita that's been layered in the bowl with a cream of condensed milk, nuts, and red bean paste. At the table we have to mix the different layers of the green granita together and then ladle it into small bowls for each other. Sharing really plays an important role in eating here. Perhaps we should do it more often in Germany, because you learn to pay attention to other people and give something of yourself while eating.

We've come to the end of our food tour. We say goodbye to each other full and happy, and everyone is glad to have met each other. I return to the hotel, feeling good, knowing that another day has passed in which I've learned a lot about my place of birth.

Day 7, April 12th. The fish market, a luxury supermarket and Michelin-starred restaurants. The day begins with a visit to Seoul's largest fish market, the Noryangjin Fish Market. It's open 24 hours a day. Three o'clock in the morning is the best time for shoppers, because that's when there's the widest selection. But I'm glad we arrived a lot later. That gives me a better chance to survey everything.

Amazing and disconcerting. The market is divided into an old and a new fish hall. Unfortunately, the old hall is half empty because many stands have already moved to the new hall. That's a shame because the old hall is a lot more charming. The fish and clams are neatly lined up at each stand, and cold water is continuously poured over them. Many vendors have small aquariums in which live fish swim, something I saw in Busan too. Several stands offer the same regional products. But there's still an incredible variety, and I see a lot of products that I've never seen before, or at least not "in the flesh": small octopus, bright yellow and red fish (perhaps a type of bream?), eels, monkfish, rays, snow crabs, shrimp of all sizes and colors, sea urchins, all sorts of clams and sea snails, sea cucumbers, scallops, crabs, and fish that I can't even identify.

The new market hall is a lesson in visual contrasts. Monitors hang above the stands and display the name and telephone number of the respective vendor. The products on offer are similar to those available in the old hall, except that the fishmongers here are obviously younger, and everything looks more organized. The water basins are arranged like a staircase, probably to make full use of the small space for which the vendors pay a fairly high rent.

I have a somewhat disconcerting experience on the second floor of the market, where, as in other fish markets in Korea, you can select your fish and then have it prepared straight away. If it's a small eel, then the skin is peeled off while they're still alive. The fish you've selected is brought to the table, and either placed on the grill plate or in the hot broth. It doesn't get any fresher than that! Preparing an animal while it's still alive is something I'd never do, though.

.

Cheese in a luxury supermarket. After the fish market, we enter a completely different world. We visit a luxury supermarket. It feels like there's one salesperson for every five customers. In terms of appearance, everything is impeccably displayed and presented. Their fruit and vegetable department is impressive. I visted a market like this before when I was in a luxury mall in Bangkok, so I don't linger in this one. I head to the cheese department, something of a rarity in Asia. And the prices are just as precious. If I wanted to make a nice little raclette, the occasion would have to be a very special one: 7 oz (200 g) of raclette cheese costs about twelve dollars. Thank goodness the country offers enough other products that you might be able to do without raclette after all. I feel a lot more comfortable in the small china shop that Jain then directs me to. There's beautiful, simple, and very elegant porcelain here. Jain says that a lot of Michelin-starred restaurants buy their table settings here. Later, when I do visit some of them, I recognize the plates sold here by their refined filagree designs. Speaking of Michelin-starred restaurants, next up on the agenda is visiting two of them. If you go on a trip billed as a Michelin-starred chef, you had better visit your colleagues.

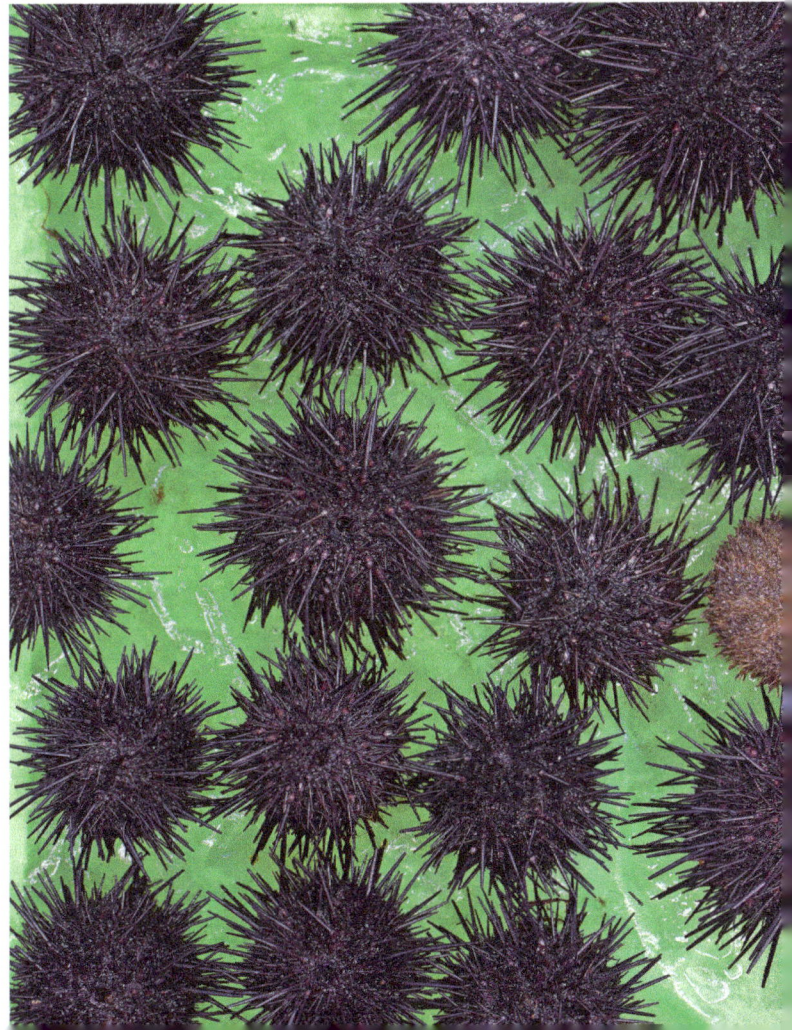

The first Michelin-starred restaurant – culinary bliss. We head to lunch at Exquisine (1 Michelin star). Exquisine is a small restaurant off the main street in the Gangnam district, a hip district in which many luxury labels and a few Michelin-starred restaurants are located. Chef Won explains that it's only been about ten years since fine dining has become more established in Korea. My first impression of Exquisine: It's exactly the kind of restaurant that I like: small and simple, with personal and very friendly service. The name is an amalgamation of "exquisite" and "cuisine," a play on words that I can confirm after my visit.

Exquisine serves cuisine in a fun atmosphere that puts you in a good mood. It starts at the table. Envelopes sealed with the restaurant's logo containing the menu are placed at each seat. It's a personal gesture that I like a lot. The servers, two young women, have a calm and friendly demeanor that they maintain throughout the evening. They convey the first "greetings from the kitchen." As a chef and restaurateur, I notice personal details like that. A peek into the kitchen: It's very small, significantly smaller than mine at Yoso. I count three cooks, which is about right for five tables. Exquisine offers a four-course lunch menu for the equivalent of around 38 dollars, an absolutely fair price, if not too little, for what we are about to get.

We start with three small amuse-bouches: a mini-omelette roll, filled with crab salad and garnished with grapefruit; a baby spinach leaf with raw ham and a piece of pickled daikon; a rice and quinoa crunch; and as the third, a baked quail egg rolled in ground, roasted perilla seeds, garnished with tiny dried and caramelized shrimps and a very finely flavored ssamjang paste. I'm really excited and am looking forward to the first course: green asparagus, which, like ours in Germany, is grown seasonally in Korea. Since it's currently in season, I will get to try in it in a variety of ways in the next two Michelin-starred restaurants as well. In Germany, we have a similar seasonal fixation on asparagus, only it's the white variety, not the green one.

I get two green versions here — one grilled, with distinct grill flavors, and one boiled. Both versions are garnished with herbs, a small meringue, a grated light powder and red chili powder. Everything is not only beautiful in terms of presentation, but also well-combined in terms of taste, and it's served with seared langostino. The kitchen sends us an extra course because Jain revealed when I made the reservation that I'm a Michelin-starred chef from Germany. It's a nice gesture that I also like to do for colleagues. It's also super delicious and makes me completely forget that I'm not a fan of sea urchins. Sea urchin butter is grated over lettuce leaves and a very elaborately wrapped potato cream. There are also pickled pearl onions for acidity, which perfectly absorb the heaviness of the butter. The potato cream in the baked crunchy coating tastes really intense like potatoes and is nice and crispy. I absolutely love this dish.

The next course is a soup with pearl barley, abalone, and small octopi, just the thing for me as someone who loves soup. For the main course, you can choose between duck or beef, and I go for the dry-aged duck breast, as I've never tried

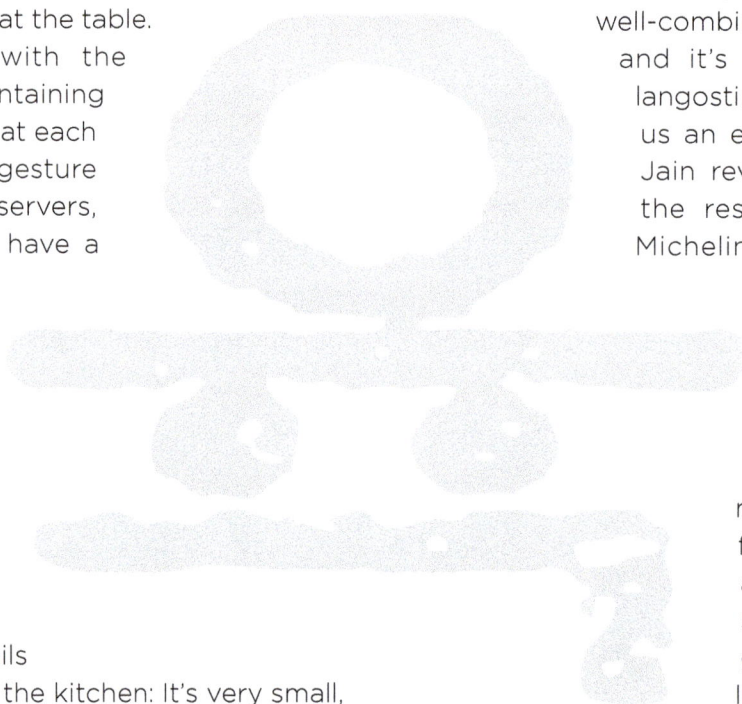

duck breast in this form before. It's been aged for three weeks and is incredibly tender with a very crisp skin. It's served with fried oyster mushrooms and pickled shimeji mushrooms. The sauce is strong and contains a few leaves from the lemony Szechuan bush (I have to pick some leaves from the bush before I leave and take them with me). All in all, it's a great main course that satiates, but like everything here, it goes down smoothly; it doesn't "fill you up" too much. The dessert is an interpretation of popcorn with mulberries. A sweet ending.

I also get to know Chef Won personally. I try to explain to him with my basic knowledge of English that I'm very impressed with his food, and that I see a parallel to my philosophy in the kitchen. A balanced play of textures and consistencies and an exact harmony between sweetness, acidity, spiciness, and umami, and using, whenever possible, regional products in a unique way. A kitchen with a lot of heart. He seems pleased that I describe and experience his way in the kitchen like this. Maybe he'll be able to visit me in Andernach and we can cook for the guests together. He responds enthusiastically when I propose that he provide a recipe for the planned cookbook. Sadly, that didn't work out in the end.

Completely satisfied and inspired by the good food, we say goodbye, and continue on to a "culinary school" where I can taste five different rice wines/schnapps in the afternoon. I take a sip from each one, but quickly realize that they're not to my taste. Jain and I go to another tea house to take a break before we take a taxi to the hotel to change clothes and then back to the Gangnam district. Our destination is the restaurant Mingles, which is number eleven in the list of "Asia's 50 Best Restaurants" and currently ranked 78th among the best restaurants in the world.

Michelin-starred restaurant number two – near perfection. Mingles is larger than Exquisine and is also more hip and stylish. The service is extremely professional. I can see part of the kitchen from our table; it's separated from the actual dining area by a service area and a bar where you can also eat.

The menu starts with three perfectly prepared and flavored snacks: kiwi as part of a kind of tart; octopus hidden under daikon triangles; and egg with spinach. Then the kitchen sends us an additional amuse-bouche: an excellent tuna sashimi. This is followed by a small starter with seasonal cabbage and abalone. Perfect! A course with two kinds of vegetables comes next: green asparagus with a spicy red sauce and green oil. A second plate has carefully cut zucchini and carrot strips with a vegetable stock poured over them. Everything is kept pure. On a third plate, there's a kind of miniature muffin made from rice flour. The first fish course is "Jeju Island," a tempura-battered fish with fresh truffle. The second fish course is a white fish that's poached to perfection. It's followed by a classic Mingles dish: "jang noodles" – spaghetti with sepia and seafood. Pickled red onions give it a little kick of freshness. Perfectly plated, perfectly seasoned. Before the main course arrives, there's yet another dish: a small bowl with tartare, eel, and tapioca crisps.

Traditionally, a sorbet was served before the main course to cleanse the palate. Instead of sorbet, though, we're served in a small bowl, something called "omija tea" a traditional tea made from dried Schisandra berries. It combines the five categories of taste: sweet, sour, bitter, salty, and umami. When ordering from the tasting menu, I chose the beef for the main course. It arrives as a perfectly cooked piece of beef filet, along with a potato puree, green asparagus, a kind of bimi ("asparagus broccoli"), and fried mushrooms. The sauce is a thickened bouillon. To add a little more Korean flavor to the meal, there's also a side dish of sweet and sour pickled cucumber slices with sesame seeds.

The next course is a rice course. It consists of two components: a piece of sushi roll, green asparagus, and rice, all neatly rolled into a sheet of special green seaweed and a bowl of green seaweed soup with a sort of slippery consistency. It tastes like a slightly salty seaweed. To be honest, the consistency prevents me from finishing this soup. I'm looking forward to the dessert because it sounds interesting: crème brûlée, black rice and pecans, with pastes that are more likely to be associated with spicy cuisine, including fermented soybean paste, red pepper paste, and soybean sauce. The spicy flavors are wonderfully integrated into the sweetness of crème brûlée, black rice, and pecans.

After the meal, I'm allowed to take a photo with head chef Mingoo Kang in his kitchen. He's a very friendly, calm, and humble person. We talk briefly about my trip and about my planned visit tomorrow with a Buddhist monk and philosopher chef Jeong Kwan. Kang says he knows her well because he visits her often and, as he puts it, learns from her. That of course makes the prospect of this visit even more interesting for me. I'm more than a little satisfied with my second experience in a Michelin-starred kitchen in Korea, and I am looking forward to tomorrow.

Dakgangjeong
Crispy Fried Chicken

닭 강정

Serves 4 | Prep time: 2 ½ hours

For the dakgangjeong

1 tablespoon white sesame
  seeds

4 cloves garlic

2-3 dried red chili peppers

2 tablespoons sesame oil

¼ cup (60 mL) soy sauce

½ cup (120 mL) rice syrup

1 tablespoon white wine
  vinegar

1 tablespoon medium-hot
  mustard (if desired)

1 tablespoon brown sugar

3 lb (1.5 kg) chicken wings
  and drumsticks

1/2 teaspoon salt

Freshly ground black
  pepper

1 tablespoon freshly grated
  ginger

½ cup (60 g) cornstarch

1 quart neutral vegetable oil
  for frying

¼ cup (30 g) peanuts (if
  desired)

Dakgangjeong

Toast the white sesame seeds in a non-stick pan, without oil.

To make the seasoning sauce, mince the garlic. Remove the seeds from the chili peppers and finely chop. Heat the oil in a pan. Sweat the garlic and chili peppers in the oil. Deglaze the pan with the soy sauce, rice syrup, and vinegar and season with the mustard and sugar. Let the sauce simmer for a while, stirring occasionally, until it has thickened, then set the sauce aside.

Trim the excess skin from the chicken and put in a large bowl. Add the ginger and season with salt and pepper. Add cornstarch to the bowl and mix well until all of the pieces are well coated. Pour the vegetable oil in a large pot until it is about ¾" deep and heat to 350°F. Gently place the coated chicken pieces in the hot oil and working in batches fry the chicken for about 12 minutes each, turning each piece halfway through. Remove and set the chicken on a wire rack or a paper towel-lined plate to drain and cool. Reheat the oil to 350°F and fry the cooled chicken pieces for a second time, again working in batches for another 6 minutes until golden brown, turning halfway through. Remove and set the fried chicken pieces on a wire rack or a paper towel-lined plate to drain. Place fried chicken in a large bowl.

Fry the peanuts briefly, drain, and roughly chop. Heat the seasoning sauce in a small saucepan, stir in the peanuts and pour over the chicken pieces and gently mix until chicken is coated completely with the sauce.

To serve

Arrange the fried chicken on a platter and garnish with the toasted sesame seeds.

Gogi-gui
Korean Barbecue with Beef

고기 구이

Serves 4 | Prep time: **20 minutes** | Marinating time: **30 minutes**

For the gogi-gui

1 Asian pear

2 onions

8 cloves garlic

3 green onions

3 ½ tablespoons freshly
grated ginger

4 tablespoons soy sauce

4 tablespoons brown sugar

Freshly ground black
pepper

1 tablespoon toasted
sesame oil

2 lb (1 kg) beef tenderloin
or ribs

To serve

Grilled mushrooms
Different kinds of kimchi
Sauces
Cooked rice

Gogi-gui

For the marinade, peel the pear and grate it finely. Mince the onion and garlic. Rinse, trim the root end, and finely chop the green onions.

In a large bowl, mix the onions, garlic, green onions, pear puree, ginger, soy sauce, sugar, a little pepper, and sesame oil well until the sugar has dissolved.

With a sharp knife, cut the beef tenderloin into very thin strips and add to the bowl with the marinade. Stir, making sure that the beef is completely coated with the marinade. Cover and let marinate for at least 30 minutes.

Prepare and preheat a grill to medium-high heat. Add the marinated meat and cook about 2-3 minutes on each side.

To serve

Serve the grilled meat with any side dishes you want.

Jjamppong
Spicy Seafood Noodle Soup

짬뽕

Serves 4 | Prep time: **40 minutes**

For the jjamppong

¼ lb (120 g) lean pork loin

1 large calamari tube (fresh or frozen)

12 raw shrimp

10 cooked mussels (in the shells)

½ lb (300 g) Napa or Chinese cabbage

1/3 lb (200 g) white cabbage

1 bunch green onions

1 leek

1 carrot

3 ½ oz (100 g) mushrooms

1 onion

8 cloves garlic

1 bunch garlic chives

1 1/2 teaspoons gochugaru (Korean chili flakes)

1 tablespoon sesame oil

2 tablespoons neutral vegetable oil

2 tablespoons freshly grated ginger

Some bamboo shoots (from a can)

1 ½ quarts (1.5 L) chicken stock

1 tablespoon oyster sauce

Freshly ground black pepper

Salt

9 oz (250 g) Asian wheat noodles

Jjamppong

Cut the pork into thin strips. Cut the calamari tube lengthwise and score the inside in a crosshatch pattern. Cut it into pieces. Peel and devein the shrimp. Carefully clean the mussels. Rinse and chop the Napa or Chinese cabbage, white cabbage, green onions, and leek. Clean and finely dice the carrot. Clean the mushrooms and cut into slices. Mince the onion and garlic. Clean and roughly chop the garlic chives.

Mix the chili flakes with the sesame oil to make the seasoning mix.

Heat the vegetable oil in a pan with a high rim. Fry the garlic, ginger, and onions in the oil until golden brown, then add the meat, Napa or Chinese cabbage, white cabbage, carrot, green onions, leek, mushrooms, and bamboo shoots to the hot pan one after the other and cook while constantly stirring. Pour the seasoning mixture over the contents of the pan and stir. Add the calamari pieces and shrimp and cook 1-2 minutes more. Pour in the chicken stock and add the mussels. Season the soup with the oyster sauce and let it simmer gently, removing any foam.

Season to taste with pepper before serving.

While the soup is simmering, bring a pot of salted water to a boil. Add the wheat noodles and cook according to the instructions on the package. Drain the noodles in a colander.

To serve

Evenly portion out pasta into 4 deep bowls and ladle the soup over them.

TIP

For a milder version, leave out the chili seasoning mix and the white cabbage. To season, add 1 tablespoon fish sauce and the oyster sauce.

If you use uncooked pasta, prepare it as described on page 172 and let it simmer 5 minutes in the soupbefore serving.

Kkanpunggi
Spicy Garlic Fried Chicken

깐 풍 기

Serves 4 | Prep time: **40 minutes** | Marinating time: **15 minutes**

For the kkanpunggi

1 lb (600 g) skinless, boneless chicken breasts
3 tablespoons rice wine
3 tablespoons soy sauce
Sea salt
Freshly ground black pepper
2 dried red chili peppers
2 green onions
1 small onion
3 garlic cloves
2 tablespoons sesame oil (use chili oil for more spice)
2 tablespoons rice vinegar
2 tablespoons oyster sauce
2 teaspoons liquid honey
1 tablespoon toasted sesame oil
1 tablespoon lime juice
2/3 cup (80 g) cornstarch
1 egg white
1 quart neutral vegetable oil for frying
1 egg white

Kkanpunggi

Cut the chicken breast into 1-inch bite-size pieces and put them in a bowl. Mix 1 tablespoon rice wine, 1 tablespoon soy sauce and a little salt and pepper and pour over the chicken pieces. Stir well so that the chicken is completely covered with the marinade. Cover and let marinate in the refrigerator for at least 15 minutes. Remove the seeds from the dried chili peppers and finely chop. Rinse, trim the root end, and finely chop the green onions. Mince the onion and garlic.

In a saucepan, heat the sesame oil over medium heat and cook the chili peppers and green onions for about 1-2 minutes. Remove the chili peppers and green onions only and either throw them away or use them again later (depending on the degree of heat required).

In the same saucepan, cook the onion and garlic in the remaining oil for 1-2 minutes, until fragrant. Then stir in the rice vinegar, 2 tablespoons soy sauce, the oyster sauce, honey, 2 tablespoons rice wine, the toasted sesame oil, and the lime juice. Simmer for 4-5 minutes or until the sauce has thickened.

Mix the cornstarch with the egg white. Pour it over the marinated chicken and mix well.

In a large pot, heat the vegetable oil over medium-high heat to 350°F. Cooking in batches, carefully place the coated chicken in the hot oil and fry until crisp and golden brown, approx 3-4 minutes. Drain the fried chicken cubes on paper towels. In a large bowl, add fried chicken cubes and pour the sauce over it. Mix gently until all the chicken is evenly coated with the sauce.

To serve

Arrange the fried chicken cubes coated with the sauce on plates and serve immediately.

Samgyetang
Ginseng Chicken Soup

삼계탕

Serves 4 | Prep time: **60 minutes** | Marinating time: **30 minutes**

For the samgyetang
1 ¾ cups (330 g) round
  grain rice
4 Cornish game hens (½ lb
  / 300 g) each or 1-2 lb (1.2
  kg) whole chicken
8 cloves garlic
4 ginseng roots
8 chestnuts
8 dried jujube fruits (Korean
  dates)
Sea salt
Freshly ground black
  pepper
1 bunch green onions

Samgyetang
Put the rice in a fine-mesh strainer, rinse under cold running water, then put in a bowl, cover with cold water and soak for 30 minutes. Put the soaked rice back in the fine-mesh strainer and drain well.

Thoroughly rinse the game hens (or the chicken) inside and out under running cold water. Trim off any excess fat. Peel the garlic cloves. Scrape off the peel of the ginseng roots with a knife. Rinse the chestnuts and jujube fruits. Season the game hens (or chicken) with a little sea salt and pepper. Fill the cavities with the rice, two cloves of garlic, two chestnuts each, one ginseng root each and two jujube fruits each, then tie the legs of the spring chickens together with kitchen twine to close the abdominal cavity.

Place the game hens side by side (or the chicken by itself) in a large pot and cover with water. Rinse, trim the root end, and finely slice the green onions. Add half of the green onions to the pot. Cover with a lid and bring to a boil. Simmer for 40 minutes. (If you are using a whole chicken, increase the cooking time to around 60 minutes.) or until internal temperature reaches 165°F.

To serve
Place each stuffed game hen and some broth in a small bowl and garnish with the remaining green onions.

Yangnyeom-tongdak Sweet and Spicy Fried Chicken

양념 통닭

Serves 4 | Prep time: 2 hours

For the yangnyeom-tongdak
5 garlic cloves
1 tablespoon corn oil
2 tablespoons freshly grated ginger
4 tablespoons gochujang (spicy Korean chili paste)
1 tablespoon gochugaru (Korean chili flakes)
4 tablespoons rice syrup or brown sugar
1 tablespoon toasted sesame oil
4 tablespoons rice vinegar
1 tablespoon mirin (rice wine)
3 lb (1.5 kg) chicken wings and drumsticks
1/3 cup (40 g) cornstarch
1/3 cup (40 g) cake flour
¼ cup (30 g) glutinous rice flour
1/2 teaspoon baking powder
Sea salt
1 egg
Freshly ground black pepper
1 quart neutral vegetable oil for frying

To serve
Spicy sauce (if desired)

Yangnyeom-tongdak

To make the sauce, mince the garlic cloves. Heat the corn oil in a saucepan. Sweat the garlic and ginger in it until they are translucent. Stir in the spice paste, chili flakes, rice syrup, toasted sesame oil, rice vinegar, and mirin and simmer gently for 6 to 8 minutes, stirring occasionally until sauce has reduced and reached a syrup-like consistency. Remove the saucepan from heat and set aside.

Rinse the chicken pieces and carefully pat dry. In a large bowl, mix the cornstarch, flour, and glutinous rice flour with the baking powder, 2 teaspoons of sea salt, and the beaten egg. Season with salt and pepper. Add chicken to bowl and stir, making sure all the pieces are coated with the flour/cornstarch mixture.

In a large pot, heat vegetable oil over medium-high heat to 350°F. Gently place the coated chicken pieces in the hot oil and, working in batches, fry the chicken for about 12 minutes each, turning each piece over halfway through. Remove and set the chicken on a wire rack or a paper towel-lined plate to drain and cool. Reheat the oil to 350°F and fry the cooled chicken pieces for a second time, again working in batches for another 6 minutes until golden brown, turning halfway through. Remove and set the fried chicken pieces on a wire rack or a paper towel-lined plate to drain. Place fried chicken in a large bowl.

Reheat the sauce and pour over the chicken. Mix gently and serve immediately.

To serve
Arrange the fried chicken in bowls and serve with the spicy sauce.

SEOUL

Two days alone –
without Jain

Day 8, April 13th. The next two days are planned without a guide. I miss Jain already. But she has assured me that I can call her at any time if I need help, which makes me feel better. Since we only walked through the Namdaemun Market two days ago without paying attention to many details, I've decided to do it today and maybe buy a few things that I can take home with me. I find a few useful little things on the fourth floor of the department store, where all the kitchen utensils are located.

Then I plan to grab some breakfast — I could really get used to the warm selections here. I start with three kinds of spicy steamed dumplings: with kimchi, with chicken, and with pork. In contrast to the Chinese steamed buns, the fillings in Korea are often mixed with glass noodles. Because I'm such a soup fan, I also go looking for the booth where I had breakfast with Jain two days ago. Unfortunately, the market is so big that I feel like I'm walking in circles. Or has the alley just disappeared? Fortunately, there are alternatives, and I can get my noodle soup for the equivalent of about 80 cents.

Bolstered by my hearty breakfast, I'm brave enough to go on a brief journey into my past, because on a Korean city map app, Jain marked the two places that I knew about from my past. The children's home I was in before I came to Germany and the police station I was taken to when they found me. I want to go there today. I feel a little sad and strange. It's another one of those moments when I wish Christian were with me. Everything on this trip is very exciting and there are so many impressions that I would love to share with him, but it's right now that I miss him the most. The area where the police station is located is very busy. Thanks to the free Wi-Fi that Seoul offers in many areas of the city, I find the station quickly. It's a small building right in the middle of everything. Across the street, there's a place to sit : The seats — probably designed by artists — are made of different materials and shapes to allow you to take a short break from shopping. For me, it's an opportunity to pause and take a deep breath. I'm sitting across from a piece of the past. So strange. I'm again imagining endless scenarios or reasons for why I might have been wandering around alone in Seoul back then... I'll probably never know. I was brought here 34 years ago. This is the first location of my life for which there's an official record. For most people, such a place is the hospital where they were born; for me it's a police station that someone brought me to when I was one and a half years old. Everything that happened before that is uncertain. Talking about it is difficult. It's hard to put into words what I feel and what preoccupies me. Somehow, I'm sad and at the same time happy that I had the courage to come here. By myself: just like I did 34 years ago.

It's only just now that I really notice how much I've already learned, experienced, and discovered on this trip. I went to Korea to learn as much as possible from the country I was born in. There are thousands of impressions that I'm taking in every day. Sounds, smells, colors... And the same question always goes through my head: What would my life have been like if I had grown up here? The more I play it over in my mind, the more upset I get. So I decide to seek a distraction from it all. I visit a cat café.

The Cat Café – What will they think of next?
The Koreans are kind of crazy. I saw the sign for my next destination on the way back from the "O'ngo Food" cooking class and decided to take a closer look today: "Cat Café". It turns out to be a kind of mini-mini-zoo. Following the instructions on a notice board in front of the entrance, I take off my shoes and put on the provided plastic slippers. After entering the room, I disinfect my hands, put all of my private items in a plastic bag, and stow it under the bench. I pay the entrance fee and get a ticket — and a free drink. I then enter the actual "café": a large room with many places of retreat for the

20 or so cats of different breeds that live there, some of them prettier, some less so. If you want to pet the cats, you can buy a treat to attract them. I decide to sit on the bench and watch. A family with four children is clearly having fun feeding the animals. After finishing my drink and taking a few photos, I leave this crazy place — and look forward to seeing my two cats at home in Germany.

Street food at Gwangjang Market. Jain wrote down a few places that I might find interesting. Of course, I'm most interested in the hotspots for food, so my next destination is Gwangjang Market. Since it's now about 6 p.m., right before rush hour, I decide to go there on foot. It's also very easy to find, because you just have to follow the Cheonggyecheon Stream, which has been converted into a park-like recreation facility. This park is also a wonderfully peaceful haven amidst the bustling big city.

The entrance into the Gwangjang Market greets me with col- ored lights and lots of people. The first thing I do is try to get a general overview of the whole place. I'm eager to verify my guidebooks' claim that the best street food in Seoul could be found here. An old woman waves me over and greets me in Korean. When I smile instead of saying anything in reply, she quickly intuits that I don't understand a word and hands me a very worn English-language menu. I'm somehow able to make her understand that I would like to have a little bit of everything. She is thrilled and starts to put things on the table. Everything is served on plastic plates, which are, in turn, wrapped in a plastic bag. This saves them from having to wash up afterwards, as the plastic bags and the leftovers go in the trash. I really don't feel like thinking about that right now. There are sliced pig's feet (trotters), ox bone soup, chicken feet, and black pudding. The sight of the chicken feet makes me hesistate a bit; it takes no small effort merely to try them. I don't really care for their gristly consistency. Still, of the four dishes, they taste the best. I probably won't order the other three things again either, because I've eaten other Korean dishes on this trip that I like a lot better. To compensate for the unsatisfying experience, I order a seafood pancake at a different stand. It's really greasy, but delicious.

"Dog Soup" – Seriously?! I saw a small sign on the way to the pancake stand advertising "dog soup," in other words soup that includes dog meat as its primary ingredient. When we meet again, I ask Jain if this is actually a thing, and she says that "dog soup" used to be eaten a lot, mainly because it was very healthy. Her family also made it at home. But since the preparation is now a legal gray area, it's hard to find these days. And since dogs have become a beloved pet in Korea, the soup is no longer very popular with the younger generations. For me, who only know dogs as pets, this is all extremely upsetting. With Jain's explanations, in hindsight the scene in front of the "dog soup" bar looks even more bizarre, because now I recall that there was a dog tied up to the stand next to it. I hope that it belonged to a guest and went home with them again. But there's a reason why people say "other countries, other customs," which I have not always understood. I go back to the hotel with these fresh impressions of Korea. It's not that late yet, so there are still a lot of people sitting in the restaurants that I go past. But even in Korea the streets are not open 24/7; the later it gets, the quieter it gets.

Day 9, April 14th. Exploring Seoul. Since I survived the first day without Jain, I'm looking forward to discovering new things again today, and even though I rarely have breakfast at home, I just have to have a warm soup here. Unfortunately, it's a bit rainy today, so I buy an umbrella in the first souvenir shop I come across. It's totally overpriced, just as they are in shops like these the world over. At least it's small enough to take back to Germany. Yet another souvenir.

I set off for Pagoda Park, another place I was 34 years ago. I've been talking to my parents on the phone regularly during my trip, and my father told me a few places they'd gone with me in the ten days we spent here together. Pagoda Park, now called Tapgol Park, is a very small park from the Joseon Dynasty and was once the site of Weongaksa (the Buddhist temple). It's known for a seven-story pagoda from this period, which is protected under glass. Of course, I can't remember having been here before.

On the way there I also find a small soup place and order "kimchi soup," which comes with a bowl of rice and an additional bowl of kimchi. At the entrance you can take water from a water dispenser free of charge. I'm sitting in a row of tables with two older men. They make an incredible racket while consuming their food. It's incredible the sorts of noises that can come from a person. But they seem to be enjoying their meal.

After visiting Pagoda Park, I go back to Changgyeonggung Palace. Since the weather is not as inviting today, there are only a few people on the grounds, which I find very pleasant. And that's how one of the most beautiful pictures of my trip came to be taken: it's a stone path flanked by old trees and walls from the palace grounds. This picture represents the path that undertaking this journey has meant for me. I'm feeling a little proud of myself.

Filling the lunch box. I continue on to the Tongin Market where you can buy a lunch box and coins, then go through the market and fill your lunch box for whatever your coins can buy. As I did at the previous market, I start by getting a general overview of the market, because this strategy has proven itself useful. I observe everything around me. There are many families with children here, and the children are obviously having fun choosing all the different dishes and paying with the coins themselves. Unfortunately, I discover that the market is a lot of fun, but that the food is not particularly good. Maybe I just ordered the wrong dishes?

I head back to "my" district of Insa-dong. It's only now that I notice that there are a lot of small souvenir shops here. I decide to soak in the atmosphere and simply let myself be carried away a bit into the flow of the other visitors. There are souvenirs such as Korean handicrafts, masks, porcelain tea sets, bags, and much more that are suitable as typical souvenirs or mementos.

Food trucks – too western. Our guide on the food tour two days ago, said that there are six places in Seoul that you can find food trucks, so I'm going to find one — mostly because I'm curious about how they differ from food trucks in Europe. I'm a bit disappointed, because they mostly offer Western products, from different sorts of hot dogs to schnitzel and sweet-and-sour burgers (at least there's that!). But most of them have steaks with potato wedges, coleslaw, red cabbage, and lettuce. Since I'm not especially interested in trying Korean takes on Western fare, I make my way back to the hotel.

I hear music and see a stage where many spectators are standing and three boys who are dancing on the stage are being filmed in front of a shopping center. There are four girls in front of the next shopping center, but the crowd was much larger for the boys. Of course, I have no idea whether the boys or the girls are famous or newcomers who are getting their big break. However, I can't avoid visiting one of the shopping centers and viewing it from the inside, and because I've heard that Denmark and Korea are fashion trendsetters, I buy a few things to bring home. I wonder if these will be in fashion next year?

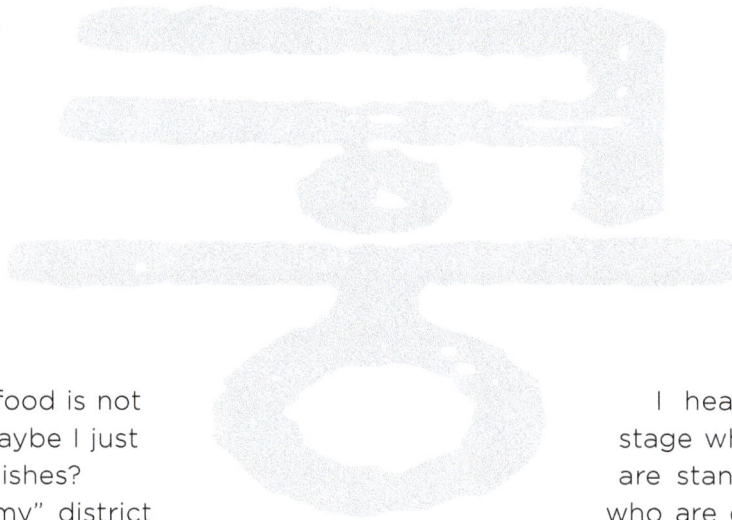

Haemul pajeon
Seafood Scallion Pancake

해물파전

Serves 4 | Prep time: 60 minutes | Marinating time: 30 minutes

For the haemul pajeon
1 tablespoon white sesame
  seeds
4 cloves garlic
¾ -1 lb (400 g) mixed
  seafood
(calamari, shrimp)
1 tablespoon toasted
  sesame oil
Salt
Freshly ground black
  pepper
2 bunches green onions
1 green chili pepper
1 red chili pepper
3 1/3 cups (400 g) cake
  flour
½ cup (50 g) glutinous rice,
  flour, or cornstarch
4 eggs
4 tablespoons neutral
  vegetable oil

For the dip (if desired)
4 tablespoons soy sauce
2 teaspoons rice vinegar
1 teaspoon toasted sesame
  oil
1 clove of garlic
½ teaspoon white sesame
  seeds

Haemul pajeon
Toast the sesame seeds in a non-stick pan, without oil. Mince the garlic. Clean the seafood under running water, drain well, and place in a bowl. Add half of the garlic, the toasted sesame seeds, sesame oil, and a pinch of salt and pepper and mix well. Cover and let the seafood marinate for about 30 minutes.

Clean the green onions and cut lengthways into strips, making sure they fit the size of your skillet. Clean the chili peppers, remove the seeds, and slice into thin rings.

Mix the flour, sticky rice flour, and 1/4 teaspoon salt in a mixing bowl. In a separate bowl, whisk the eggs and add to the flour with the remaining garlic. Gradually stir in about ¾ cup of cold water and make a viscous dough.

In a pan, heat 2 tablespoons of vegetable oil over medium-high heat. Spread a third of the batter in the pan. Place half of the green onions and half of the marinated seafood on the batter. Pour some more batter onto the pancake so that it's covered. Cook on medium heat for 3–4 minutes until golden brown, then turn the pancake out onto a plate and slide it back into the pan to cook the other side until it's also golden brown. Use the remaining ingredients to cook a second pancake.

Before serving, cut the pancakes into bite-size pieces.

Dip
Mix all of the ingredients together and serve in a separate bowl.

To serve
Arrange the pancake pieces in a small bowl and serve with the dip
if desired.

Kimchi Mandu
Kimchi Dumplings

김치만두

Serves 4 | Prep time: 80 minutes | Marinating time: 30 minutes

For the kimchi mandu
3 1/3 cup (300 g) cake flour
Salt
1 clove of garlic
1/2 onion
1 tablespoon garlic chives,
  finely chopped
1 ¾ cups (250 g) kimchi (see
  "Baechu kimchi" on p. 32)
9 oz (250 g) firm tofu
2 ¾ cups (200 g) mung
  bean sprouts
¼ lb (130 g) ground pork
  or beef
1 egg
1 tablespoon toasted
  sesame oil
Freshly ground black
  pepper
Neutral vegetable oil

To serve
Sauce (as desired)

Kimchi mandu

Mix the flour with a pinch of salt and about ½ cup of water to knead it into a smooth, firm dough. Shape the dough into a ball, wrap it with cling film and let it rest in the refrigerator for 30 minutes.

Mince the garlic and onion for the filling. Drain the kimchi and finely chop. Finely chop the tofu.

Briefly blanch the mung bean sprouts in boiling water, drain, and finely chop.

Put the garlic, onions, kimchi, tofu, ground meat, bean sprouts, egg, sesame oil, and a little pepper and salt in a bowl and mix well.

Take the dough out of the cling film and put onto a lightly-floured surface, roll dough into a rope about 1-foot long and cut into 30 pieces. While you are working with the dough, cover the pieces of dough that are not being processed with a damp kitchen towel so that they do not dry out. Roll out each piece into a circular shape (approx. 3 ½-inches in diameter). Place 1 tablespoon of the filling onto the center of each round. Brush the free edges of the dough with a little water, then fold the ends together to form crescents.

To steam the mandus, bring the water to boil in a steamer pot or saucepan. Using a lined bamboo steamer, place the mandus inside, cover with a lid and steam for 15–20 minutes. (Alternatively, the mandus can also be placed in a pot of boiling salted water. Reduce
the temperature and let the mandus simmer on low for an additional 6–7 minutes.

To serve
Arrange the dumplings and serve a spicy sauce in separate bowls with it.

CCTV
작동중

광명안전
1588-1149

찐 빵
steamed bread | three ₩2,000
도우넛
nut cake

고로케 | one
croquette | ₩1,000

고기만두 | 5つ ₩3,000
肉まんじゅう
김치만두 | 10つ ₩5,000
キムチぎょうざ

찐 빵 | 3つ

모리자

기분 좋은
하루280

Facial Tissue
280매 × 3개 × 8봉

안성예절교

Dakbal
Baked Chicken Feet

닭발

Serves 4 | Prep time: 90 minutes | Marinating time: 20 minutes plus 2 hours

For the dakbal
1 lb (500 g) chicken feet
2 tablespoons coarse sea
salt
½ cup (120 mL) soju
3 cloves garlic
1–5 Thai chili peppers
2 tablespoon gochugaru
(Korean chili flakes)
1 tablespoon oyster sauce
1 tablespoon soy sauce
1 tablespoon mirin (rice
wine)
1 tablespoon toasted
sesame oil
1 tablespoon gochujang
(spicy Korean chili paste)
1 tablespoon sugar
1/3 cup (30 g) freshly
grated ginger
Freshly ground black
pepper

To serve
Green onions (if desired)

Dakbal
Clean the chicken feet, place them in a large bowl and sprinkle with the salt. Massage the salt into the chicken feet, then pour in enough water to completely cover and stir in the soju. Allow to rest for 20 minutes, then drain and rinse well under cold water. Bring water to boil in a steamer pot or saucepan. Using a lined bamboo steamer, place the chicken feet inside, cover with a lid and steam for 60 minutes.

For the seasoning sauce, mince the garlic. Clean the chili peppers, remove the seeds, and finely chop.

In a large bowl, mix the garlic, chili peppers, chili flakes, oyster sauce, soy sauce, mirin, sesame oil, spice paste, sugar, ginger, and some pepper in a bowl.

Place the cooked chicken feet in bowl with the seasoning sauce and mix well. Cover the bowl with cling film and let the chicken feet sit in the refrigerator for about 2 hours.

Preheat the oven to 350°F. Place the chicken feet side by side on a lined baking sheet and bake for about 5 minutes or until crispy. (You can also grill the chicken feet on a grill rack until crispy.)

To serve
Arrange the chicken feet on a platter and garnish with finely chopped green onions as desired. (Photo: bottom of plate on p. 159.)

TIP

"Gochugaru" or "gochutgaru" are the names of Korean chili flakes of various grinds and levels of spice. They cannot easily be replaced by another product, as they have a very unique, somewhat mild taste that's characteristic of many Korean dishes. They are available in well stocked Asian stores or on the Internet. An opened package can easily be stored in the refrigerator in an airtight container. If the flakes stick together, they can be ground with a food processor.

Sundae
Korean Blood Sausage

족발

Makes 3 blood sausages | Prep time: **90 minutes** | Marinating time: **60 min**utes

For the sundae

3 feet (1 meter) cleaned
 natural casing or plastic
 casing (order in advance
 from the butcher)
Salt
6 oz (180 g) uncooked glass
 noodles
5 green onions
1 teaspoon white sesame
 seeds
3 cloves garlic
5 cups (1 kg) cooked,
 cooled rice
2/3 cup (100 g) freshly
 grated ginger
1/2 teaspoon freshly ground
 black pepper
1 tablespoon toasted
 sesame oil
1 2/3 cup (400 mL) liquid
 beef or pig blood (order in
 advance from the butcher)

Sundae

Soak the natural casing in salt water for 1 hour (1 quart of water with 1 teaspoon of salt). Cut the soaked intestine into pieces about 1-foot long. Close one end of each casing tightly with kitchen twine.

For the filling, put the glass noodles in a bowl, pour warm water over them and soak until they are soft. Using a colander, drain the glass noodles and then roughly chop.

Rinse, trim the root end, and finely chop the green onions. Toast the sesame seeds in a pan, without oil, then crush them with a mortar and pestle.

Mince the garlic. Put the chopped glass noodles, cooked rice, green onions, ground sesame seeds, garlic, ginger, 1 teaspoon salt, pepper, toasted sesame oil, and blood or liquid beef in a large bowl and mix well.

Using either a funnel or a sausage filling machine, fill the prepared natural casings with the blood sausage mixture. Do not fill the intestines too tightly or they will burst. Once the intestines are full, close the open ends tightly with kitchen twine. Place the sausages in a large saucepan and cover completely with a salt water solution (1 quart of water and 1 teaspoon of salt). Bring the salt water to a boil and add the blood sausages, cooking for 45 minutes, then carefully pierce a sausage with a toothpick to check for doneness. If toothpick comes out clean, with no filling sticking to it, then the sausages are done. The sausages can be eaten immediately or stored in the refrigerator or freezer for later. In Korea, these blood sausages are often grilled or used as a filler in stews. (Photo: top of plate on p. 159.)

이조식당

잔치국수 Janchi-guksu (Banquet Noodles) / 宴面 / にゅうめん	**4,000**원
콩국수 Kong-guksu (Noodles in Cold Soybean Soup) / 豆浆面 / 豆乳素麺	**5,000**원
찐만두 Steamed dumplings / 蒸饺 / 蒸し餃子	**5,000**원
우무가사리 Gar-agar, Ceylon moss / 石花菜 / セイロンゴケ	**5,000**원
머리고기 meori gogi (Ox Head Slices) / 白切猪肉 / モリゴギ(牛頭肉)	**10,000**원
(Tripe) / 牛肠 / コブチャン(牛もつ)	**10,000**원
족발 Jokbal (Pigs' Feet) / 酱猪蹄 / 豚足	**8,000**원
허파 Ox lung stir-fry / 肺藥味 / 炒肺	**7,000**원
순대 Sundae (Korean Blood Sausage) / 米肠 / もち米入り豚の腸詰め	**7,000**원
닭발 Dak bal (Chicken Feet) / 鸡爪 / 鶏モミジ	**7,000**원
떡볶이 Tteok-bokki (Stir-fried Rice Cake) / 辣炒年糕 / トッポッキ	**3,000**원
오뎅 Oden (Fish Cake) / 鱼饼汤 / 練り天	**3,000**원
김밥 Gimbap (Gimbap) / 紫菜卷饭 / キンパブ	**3,000**원
짜장면 Jjangmyeon (Noodles with Black Soybean Sauce) / 炸酱面	**5,000**원

Jokbal
Braised Pig's Trotters

족발

Serves 4 | Prep time: 3 hours | Marinating time: 12 hours

For the spice bag
1 onion
8 cloves garlic
1 apple
5 green onions
8 dried jujube fruits (Korean dates)
1 tablespoon (20 g) freshly grated ginger
2-6 dried red chili peppers
1 star anise
1 teaspoon black peppercorns
1 tablespoon ground coffee

For the jokbal
4 ½ lb ((2 kg) pig's trotters
3 tablespoons (20 g) freshly grated ginger
2 tablespoons doenjang (Korean fermented soybean paste)
¼ cup (60 mL) mirin (rice wine)
½ cup (80 mL) soy sauce
½ cup (50 g) brown sugar
1 tablespoon salt
½ cup (120 mL) rice syrup
1 green onion, finely diced
1/2 teaspoon white sesame seeds

Spice bags
After the pig's trotters have soaked (see below), prepare the spice bags. Peel and roughly chop the onion and garlic. Clean the apple, cut out the core, and cut into wedges. Rinse, trim the root end, and roughly chop the green onions Pour all of the ingredients into an appropriately sized spice bag and seal.

Jokbal
Clean the trotters under running water and place in a large bowl, cover completely with cold water and soak in the refrigerator for about 12 hours, changing the water three to four times. After soaking, take the trotters out of the water, dry them well and carefully remove any bristle hairs. In a large pot, bring about 2 ½ liters of water to a boil. Add the trotters and ginger and cover. Cook for 20-25 minutes. Drain the trotters and rinse thoroughly under running water. Clean the pot and place trotters back inside.

Attach the spice bag to the edge of the pot and pour about 2 ½ quarters of water into the saucepan and stir in the soy paste, mirin, soy sauce, sugar, salt, rice syrup, chopped green onions, and sesame seeds. Put a lid on the pot and bring to a boil. Reduce the heat and cook on a medium simmer for 2 hours, turning the trotters halfway through. After 2 hours, the meat should be fork tender and almost falling off the bone. Remove the lid from the pot and simmer the trotters for another 10 minutes. While simmering, ladle the broth over the trotters repeatedly until the skin becomes browner and shinier. Place the cooked pork feet on a carving board and let cool for 15 to 20 minutes. Remove the bones and slice the meat.

To serve
Arrange the cut meat decoratively on a platter and serve.

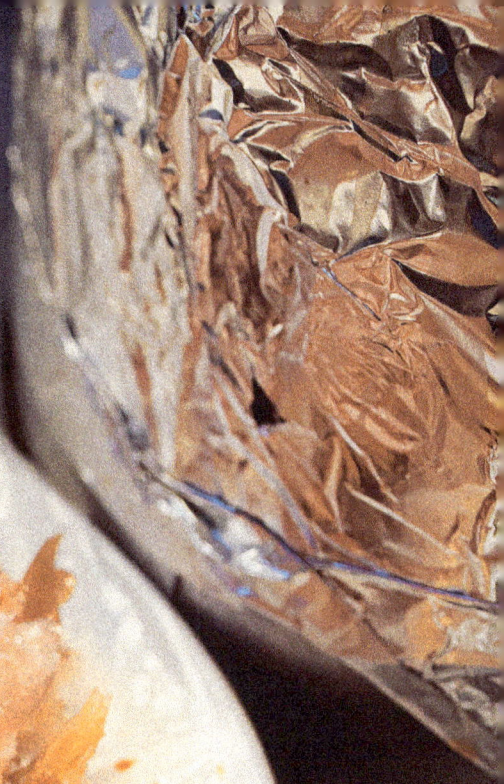

JEONJU

Historic city and cradle of the Joseon Dynasty

Day 10, April 15th. This morning we took the train from Seoul to Jeonju, which is about 140 miles south of the capital. I can meet Okjung again – this time with her son. What a sweet child! He arrives at our lunch on a mini-tricycle. Of course, we have arranged to meet for bibimbap for lunch, because Jeonju is supposed to have the best in Korea. Clearly, word has gotten out, because you can't even make reservations here. Those who come have to wait until a table becomes available. However, since the guests simply eat quickly and then leave, we don't have to wait too long. Today I choose the bibimbap with raw tartare. It's a lot spicier than all the bibimbaps I've eaten so far, and the bowl is lovingly arranged with brightly colored ingredients.

After lunch we walk to the Hanok Heritage Village with the Geonggjion Shrine. Since the weather is nice again, quite a few people are out and about, and, similar to the palace in Seoul, many of them are wearing traditional clothes, which you can also rent here. You get the impression that you're on a film set. If you leave the center of the village, the atmosphere changes completely. Narrow, serpentine-like alleyways lead to a small hill. Both sides of these alleys, which are too narrow for cars, have houses that have been painted by various artists. It looks a bit weird really, because all of these houses are pretty run down and only partially inhabited and some of them have small bars and cafés in them.

Makgeolli – rice beer with extras. Tonight, we try a very typical Korean drink that is served with many small dishes — makgeolli, a kind of rice beer. Were I on my own, I would never have even considered trying it, and if the travel guides that I read before my trip mentioned it, I may have overlooked it. We order a liter of makgeolli, which is poured out of jugs, and are then served an endless array of small dishes — so many that it's impossible to finish everything. I can only list a few of them here: pig's trotters, kimchi pancake, kimchi with pork and tofu, fried eggs, mussel soup, chicken soup, cockles, fried fish, raw crab marinated in soy sauce, fried kimchi pockets, fried enoki mushrooms and gingko berries, red shrimp cooked on salt.

We were one of the first tables in the restaurant, and half an hour later it was full and the volume had increased significantly. You can equate the noise level when eating with the level of satisfaction. As soon as people sit down at a set table, they become exuberant and fun. It doesn't matter where; there doesn't have to be a special occasion, and the food doesn't have to be as excellent as it is at this restaurant, Koreans will still toast each other, eat, and laugh. It feels great to be a part of an atmosphere of such pleasure — something I've already experienced many times during this trip. I read somewhere that Korean food connects people. I couldn't agree more!

Snacks in the supermarket. Jain leads me to our next food stop. It's unusual and certainly not something that you'd find in any travel guide: snacks in the supermarket. Jain explains that this practice, which is very popular with the locals, originated in the 1970s. If you wanted to eat with friends, but your own living room and budget were too small, then you would meet in a sales room in grocery stores, and there are still a few of these "snack bars" around. There are very few tables with chairs set up there; there is a television, shelves with chips, and instant soups. If you want, you can also just get a bag of chips and a can of beer. Or you can order small snacks that are listed on a board. Jain is incredibly excited to bring me here and immediately orders her two favorite snacks: dried octopus and a dried, crispy fish (pollack). The octopus, is pounded soft in the dining room with a wooden stick and then grilled. There's also a small, flat block of wood in the entrance area and a plastic stool in front of it where an elderly lady squats. She chars the octopus on the grill in front of her and taps the individual arms on all sides so that the body is broken up and almost fibrous. She serves us the octopus meat, cut into bite-size pieces, together with a very spicy dip. It consists of a thick teriyaki sauce and some kind of sour cream with green pepper slices, some of which are incredibly hot, as I find out. True to its original purpose, the space manages to make you feel like you are sitting in someone's living room. The atmosphere is absolutely informal, and I'm glad that I was able to be able to experience it. Gamsahamnida, Jain! Thank you, my little sister.

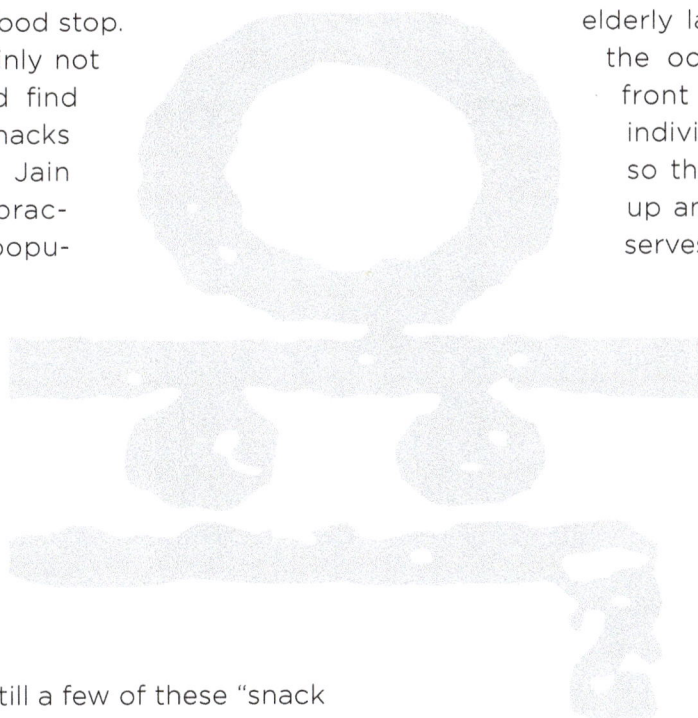

Jeonju Bibimbap

전주 비빔밥

Serves 4 | Prep time: **70 minutes** | Marinating time: **12 hours**

For the jeonju bibimbap

1 oz (30 g) gosari (dried, young fernbrake (or fiddlehead fern)
1 oz (30 g) doraji (dried bellflower root)
2/3 lb (300 g) chuck steak
1/3 lb (150 g) Asian pears
2 green onions
4 cloves garlic
1 ½ tablespoons (10 g) freshly grated ginger
Soy sauce
3 teaspoons sugar Freshly ground black pepper
5 teaspoons toasted sesame oil
2 cups (400 g) round grain rice
½ quart (450 mL) beef broth
Salt
2 tablespoons gochujang (spicy Korean chili paste)
1 tablespoon gochugaru (Korean chili flakes)
1 tablespoon rice syrup
1 tablespoon white wine vinegar
Some coarse sea salt
1 ½ cups (200 g) daikon radish
10 ½ oz / 10 cups (300 g) fresh spinach
2 ½ oz (100 g) bamboo shoots
.35 oz (10 g) wakame (dried seaweed)
Vegetable oil

Jeonju bibimbap

Place the gosari and doraji in separate bowls. Pour cold water over them and leave to soak overnight.

Cut the beef into bite-size pieces and put into a bowl. Peel the pear and finely grate it for the marinade. Rinse, trim the root end, and finely chop the green onions. Mince the garlic. For the marinade, mix the grated pear, half of the green onions, and half of the garlic with the ginger, 3 1/2 tablespoons soy sauce, 2 teaspoons of sugar, a little pepper, and the sesame oil. Pour over the beef and mix well. Cover
and let the beef marinate in the refrigerator for at least 60 minutes.

Using a fine-mesh strainer, rinse the rice three times in cold water and drain well. Place the rice in a bowl of cold water, cover with a lid and soak the rice for 30 minutes. Drain and transfer to a saucepan. Add the beef stock and bring everything to a boil in a tightly lidded saucepan. Reduce the temperature and let the rice simmer for about 7 minutes. Stir the rice vigorously once, close the pan again and simmer on low for another 3 minutes. Remove from heat and let sit for another 10 minutes. Remove lid and fluff the rice with a fork.

Drain the gosari and doraji. In a small saucepan add salt water and the gosari. Bring to a boil then reduce heat to a simmer and cook for 15-25 minutes or until soft. (The cooking time depends on the age of the gosari.) Remove from heat and drain well.

Heat 2 teaspoons of sesame oil in a skillet or pan over medium heat. Add ¼ of the remaining garlic and gently sauté until soft and translucent. Add the gosari and sauté with the garlic, then season with 1 tablespoon soy sauce and pepper.

For the Doraji marinade, in a large bowl, mix the spice paste, the chili flakes, 1/2 teaspoon soy sauce, the rice syrup, 1 teaspoon sugar, 1 pinch of salt, the vinegar, the remaining green onions, the remaining garlic, and 1 teaspoon roasted sesame oil together. Cut the softened doraji into cubes, knead briefly with coarse sea salt and rinse under running water. Drain well and add to the bowl with the marinade.

Peel the radish, cut into fine strips and blanch for 1 minute in boiling salted water. Trim the spinach and rinse well under cold running water. Gently dry the spinach using paper towels. Heat 1

teaspoon of sesame oil in a skillet or pan, add spinach, and cook until spinach is slightly wilted. Remove the spinach, drain well and season with 1/2 teaspoon of roasted sesame oil and a little soy sauce. Briefly blanch the bamboo shoots in boiling salted water and drain well. In a small bowl, soak the wakame in cold water for 5 minutes. Drain and set aside. Heat 2 tablespoons vegetable oil over medium-high heat. Add the marinated meat and stir fry until meat is nicely seared on all sides, about 5 minutes

To serve
Place the various vegetables in individual bowls and arrange in a circle. Serve meat in a deep dish and place in the middle.

Jogaetang
Spicy Clam Soup

조개탕

Serves 4 | Prep time: **25 minutes**

For the jogaetang
1 bunch green onions
4 cloves garlic
2 red chili peppers
4 teaspoons doenjang
  (Korean fermented
  soybean paste)
Sea salt
Freshly ground black
  pepper

To serve
Cooked rice

Jogaetang
Scrub and thoroughly rinse the clams under cold water. Using a strainer, drain well. Sort and discard any opened clams that do not close even after lightly tapping on them.

In a large pot of water, add clams and bring to boil over medium-high heat. Cook the clams for 5 minutes, skimming off any foam that rises to the surface with a slotted spoon or fine-mesh skimmer. Check the clams and discard any closed or broken ones.

Rinse, trim the root end, and finely chop the green onions. Mince the garlic. Clean the chili peppers, remove the seeds, and finely chop. Stir the green onions, garlic, chili peppers, and soybean paste into the large pot. Return to a boil and season with salt and pepper.

To serve
Ladle soup into 4 deep bowls, dividing clams evenly, and serve with rice.

Kimchi Jjigae
Kimchi Stew

김치찌개

Serves 4 | Prep time: 70 minutes

For the kimchi jjigae
7 dried anchovies
¾ cups (3 ½ oz / 100 g) daikon radish
5 green onions
1 sheet dried kelp (seaweed, 4" x 4")
3 ½ cups (500 g) cabbage kimchi (see "Baechu kimchi" on p. 32)
¼ cup (60 mL) kimchi liquid (see "Baechu kimchi" on p. 32)
1 medium onion
½ lb (250 g) pork belly or shoulder
Salt
2 teaspoons sugar
1 tablespoon gochujang (spicy Korean chili paste)
2 teaspoons gochugaru (Korean chili flakes)
1 teaspoon toasted sesame oil
7 oz (200 g) firm tofu

Kimchi jjigae

If needed, remove the heads and viscera of the anchovies and rinse under cool water. Peel and finely chop the radish. Rinse, trim the root end, and roughly chop green onions, setting aside half. In a large pan, mix anchovies and radish, half of the green onions, and kelp. Add 1 quart of water, bring to a boil and let simmer for about 20 minutes. Reduce the temperature and simmer on low for another 5 minutes. Pass the stock through a fine-mesh strainer into a second pot, reserving about ½ quart of the broth.

Roughly chop the kimchi and add to the pot. Mince the onion. Cut the pork into 1-inch, bite-size cubes.

Add the onion, the remaining green onions, and pork to the kimchi. Season the stew with a little salt, sugar, spice paste, chili flakes, and sesame oil, then add the reserved stock and bring to a boil. Reduce the temperature, cover the pot with a lid and simmer for about 10 minutes.

Cut the tofu into bite-size pieces and add to the stew. Put the lid back on and cook the kimchi stew for another 10–15 minutes. Before serving, season to taste with salt.

To serve
Ladle the kimchi stew in bowls and serve immediately.

TIP

Gochujang is a spicy, hot, fermented spice paste. It is made from glutinous rice flour, soybean flour, salt, barley malt powder, and its namesake, chili peppers (gochu). It is used for such things as a marinade for meat or as a dip for vegetables. It is available in well-stocked Asian stores or on the Internet.

Saejogae Cho Gochujang Cockles with Spicy Dip

새 조 개 초 고 추 장

Serves 4 | Prep time: 30 minutes | Marinating time: 2-4 hours

For the saejogae
2 lb (1 kg) fresh cockles
1 teaspoon salt
6 tablespoons rice wine

For the cho gochujang
1 small clove of garlic
2 tablespoons gochujang
   (spicy Korean chili paste)
2 tablespoon white wine
   vinegar
1 tablespoon brown sugar
1 tablespoon liquid honey
1 teaspoon white sesame
   seeds (if desired)

Cho gochujang
Mince the garlic. Mix the garlic with all the other ingredients except for the sesame seeds until the sugar and honey have completely dissolved. Stir in the cooled sesame seeds and set aside.

Saejogae
Scrub and thoroughly rinse the cockles under cold water and, using a strainer, drain well. Sort out and discard any opened cockles that do not close after lightly tapping on them.

In a large bowl dissolve the salt in 1 quart of water, add the cleaned cockles, cover and place in the refrigerator for 2-4 hours. Then, using a strainer, drain the cockles, and rinse under cold running water.

In a large pan, add the cockles and 1 quart of water. Add the cleaned cockles and the rice wine, cover. Bring to a boil. Lower the heat and let the cockles simmer for about 6-7 minutes. Using a strainer, drain the cockles and discard any closed or broken ones. Let them cool slightly.

To serve
Carefully open the shells completely and decoratively arrange the cockles on a plate. Pour the sauce into a small bowl and serve it on the plate with the cockles.

Saewoo Bokkeumbap Shrimp Fried Rice

새우 볶음밥

Serves 4 | Prep time: 30 minutes

For the saewoo bokkeumbap

1/2 green chili pepper
1/2 onion
2 cloves garlic
1 large carrot
2/3 lb (300 g) shrimp, unpeeled
3 tablespoons neutral vegetable oil
1 cup (150 g) whole kernel corn
1 tablespoon butter
2 eggs
4 cups (800 g) cooked rice, cooled
1 tablespoon butter
2 tablespoons oyster sauce
2 tablespoons soy sauce
Salt
Freshly ground black pepper

To serve

4 eggs (if desired)

Saewoo bokkeumbap

Clean the chili peppers, remove the seeds, and finely chop. Mince the onion and garlic. Peel the carrots and finely dice.

Heat 2 tablespoons of vegetable oil in a pan over medium-high heat. Add the onions and garlic and gently sautée until soft and translucent. Add the carrots and the chili pepper and cook 4-5 minutes until softened. Mix in the shrimp and corn kernels and cook for an additional 5 minutes, allowing any liquid to evaporate.

Whisk the eggs in a small bowl. In a separate pan, heat the remaining vegetable oil (1 tablespoon). Pour the eggs into it, let them cook without stirring. Using a rubber spatula, gently fold and stir the eggs, forming soft curds until eggs are soft scrambled and a little liquid remains.

To the pan with the shrimp, add the eggs, rice, butter, oyster and soy sauce. Over low heat, using a wooden spoon, mix all the ingredients until warmed through. Season to taste with salt and pepper.

To serve

Arrange the shrimp fried rice on 4 plates. If desired, you can substitute four fried eggs for the scrambled eggs. Serve fried eggs by placing on top of the rice.

Yangnyeom Gejang
Spicy Crabs

양념게장

Serves 4 | Prep time: **20 minutes** | Marinating time: **10 minutes plus 1–2 days**

For the yangnyeom gejang

8 blue crabs
2 tablespoons soju
3 tablespoons coarse sea
  salt
2 dried red chili peppers
1 small onion
5 cloves garlic
½ lb (200 g) Asian pears
1/8 cup (20 g) freshly
  grated ginger
4 ½ tablespoons (25 g)
  gochugaru (Korean chili
  pepper flakes)
1 tablespoon mirin (rice
  wine)
1 tablespoon white sesame
  seeds
1 tablespoon sugar
¼ cup (60 mL) rice syrup
1/2 teaspoon freshly ground
  black pepper

To serve

2 green onions, cleaned
  and finely chopped

Yangnyeom Gejang

Start by cleaning and preparing the crabs. If using frozen crabs first thaw by putting in cold water. Next, remove the top shell and gills. Using a kitchen brush, clean the shell. Cut the body into quarters. Rinse and drain well. Place crabs in a large bowl, pour the soju over them and sprinkle with 2 tablespoons of sea salt. Mix well and cover. Place bowl in the refrigerator for 10 minutes.

Remove the seeds from the chili peppers and roughly chop. Roughly chop the onion and garlic. Peel, core, and roughly chop the pears.

For the seasoning sauce, in a food processor put the chili peppers, onion, garlic, and pear with the ginger, chili flakes, mirin, sesame seeds, sugar, rice syrup, remaining salt (1 tablespoon), and a little pepper. Puree until the mixture resembles a sauce and there are no large chunks.

Drain and rinse crabs under running water and place in a large screw-top jar. Add the pureed seasoning sauce, mix well, and seal the jar until airtight. Place it in the refrigerator for 1–2 days.

To serve

Arrange the raw, marinated crab on a platter and garnish with the chopped green onions.

BAEKYANGSA

Visiting Jeong Kwan

Day 11, April 16th. Anyone who's seen the series "Chef's Table" on Netflix knows about Jeong Kwan. But I wasn't one of them. When I read the itinerary for this outing, I had no idea to whom it was referring when it stated: "Temple visit (Baegyangsa) and cooking class with monk Jeong Kwan." A Buddhist monk, Jeong Kwan lives at the Baegyangsa Temple and cooks for guests and students of Buddhism who stay with her for longer periods of time. The Netflix series "Chef's Table" brought her world fame, which wasn't something that she, as a Buddhist monk, had ever sought. Since then, she's inspired a lot of famous chefs. When I think about it now, I regret that we didn't have more time to talk to her and get to know more about her life. Our visit with Jeong Kwan turned out to be one of the most memorable days of my trip.

천진암

첫
발
심
했
을
때
가

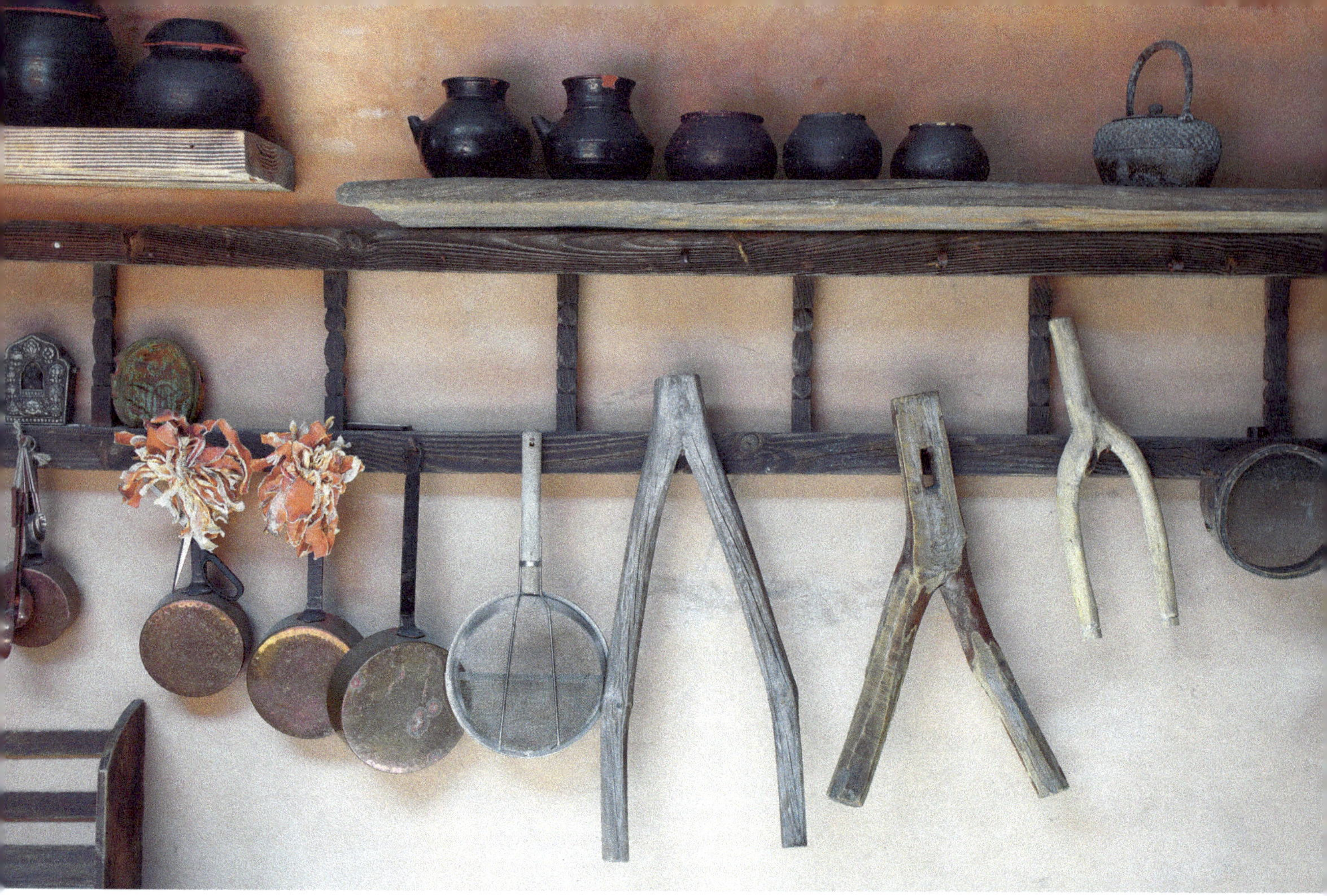

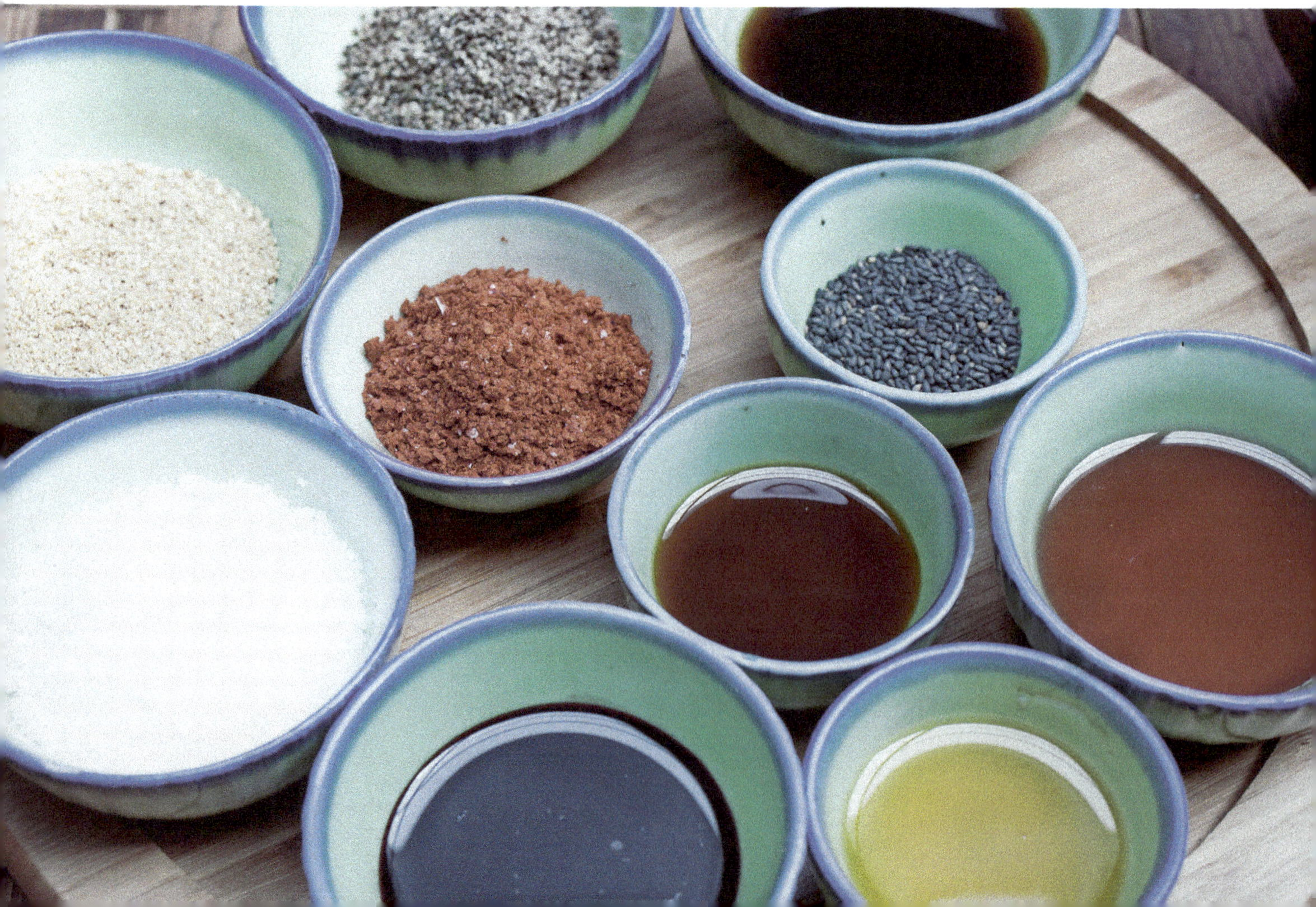

Farewelll dinner with Jain During the train ride, I ask Jain for a restaurant recommendation for my last evening in Seoul. She makes a reservation at Joo Ok, the third Michelin-starred restaurant on my trip. I'm really looking forward to this evening, because I plan to treat Jain to dinner as a small thank you for her incredible help.

It is also going to be a fantastic culinary note to end on as this eventful journey comes to an end. At Joo Ok something takes place, a little gesture of hospitality that I don't want to leave out: After we have finished our first amuse gueule, the chef sends out as a sort of welcome, something we had not ordered: a side dish of dureup. Just the day before I had picked some of these young shoots with a nutty aroma from an Angelica tree. I took the server by surprise when I interrupted his explanation, since I already knew what it was. I'm feeling pretty proud of what I've already learned during my trip about these ingredients that are new to me. But that's not the point of this story. The server explains to us that the chef picked the shoots himself, but that the harvest is too small to feature as a dish on the menu. The server then encourages us to try it (Jain had already told them who I was). The dureup is seared briefly and drizzled with roasted perilla seeds and perilla oil, and the oil is amazing! It tastes a bit like toasted sesame oil but has a much softer and finer taste. I love it so much that I ask the employee whether it is possible for the chef to tell me the brand or if I could maybe even buy a bottle of it from him. A short time later the waiter comes back and explains to me that the chef's mother-in-law makes the oil herself, so there are only a few bottles of it, but he would like to give me one. I'm caught off guard but absolutely thrilled about this very kind gesture to a colleague whom he does not know personally.

Last Day

I visited the Deoksugung Temple in Seoul yesterday, before our farewell dinner. I was also there with my parents 34 years ago. Yesterday morning, my father sent me a picture from back then, and I found the exact place where the photo had been taken. Standing there was a strange but good feeling at the same time. It was good because I was reminded that I had the courage to embark on this journey. It was strange because the trip has raised a thousand questions that will remain unanswered. A journey like this is also a journey within.

During the past few days, I haven't been a tourist who wanted to get to know the country and write a book about the food there. This was a personal trip to the country that I left as a mere toddler. My past in Korea, even if it was only brief, is part of my life. Without it, my life would not be what it is today. My life started here under circumstances that I will probably never know about. Then two people from Germany, who al- ready had two sons of their own but wanted to adopt a girl, brought me to Germany in 1984. It was perhaps only chance that brought them to Korea. For me, though, it was the best thing that could have happened to me. When they heard that they could pick me up, they came to Seoul, where I am now all these years later.

The three of us met for the first time in this city. As my family tells it, I was a "daddy's girl" from the start. We spent a few days here together, getting to know each other a bit before we went back to Germany together. I can't remember it, of course. But I know that it gave my parents the opportunity to have a brief glimpse into my home country, just like I have been able to do in the past few days.

After I briefly described the reason for my trip to Korea, Vijay, the Indian from California, whom I met on the food tour, told me that he had once had a DNA test done on himself. He was simply curious to see whether there was someone in the world with DNA similar to his. And there was! His brother! He had also had this test done but hadn't mentioned it. Vijay was relieved to find out that his DNA was similar

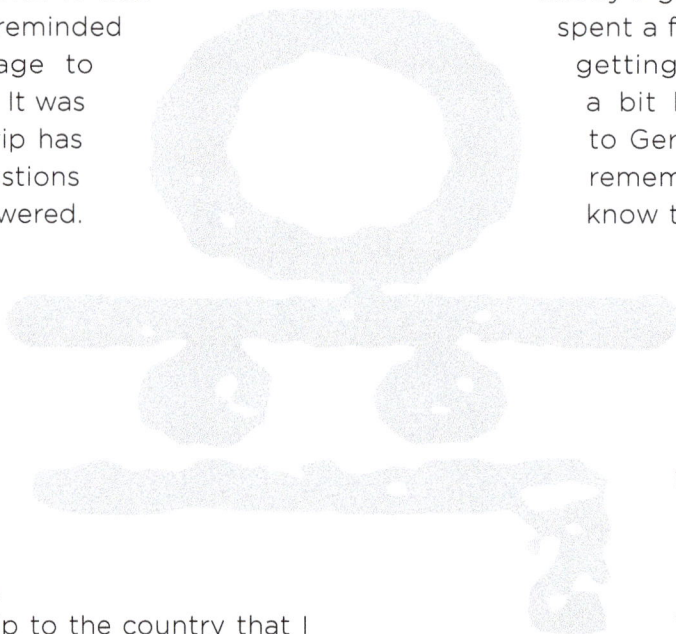

to his brother's and not to some anonymous stranger's

Not long after this conversation I thought about doing a DNA test like that, but then I decided against it. I have my family in Germany. Plus, I'm actually less afraid of whom I might find than I am of the possibility that I might not find anyone at all.

This trip has connected me with Korea in a meaningful way. That's more than enough and even more than I had expected when I set out. My plane leaves at 7:00 a.m. on the 13th day of my trip. I take the bus to the airport. The skyscrapers, the small side streets with the colorful signs, the people who are on their way to work, the many taxis, everything speeds past. My thoughts are all over the place. I'm a little sad that my time here has already come to an end and that I'm returning to my usual life. I've felt very much at home here. And even if a lot of things were new to me, there were also a few things that didn't feel strange at all or that didn't take me long to get used to. And maybe, just maybe, there is a conscious part of me that has stored all the memories of the smells, the language, and the culture.

I'm returning to Germany with a very good feeling, knowing that I've learned so much about my place of birth. I'm looking forward to creating the next menu at Yoso, inspired by all that I've learned during this trip. And I am curious to see whether I'll succeed in sharing Korean food culture with my guests.

HOME AGAIN

Recipes from Yoso and my Korean menu

Spicy stock| Sashimi | Shiitake | Lime Gelée

Serves 4 | Prep time: 2 ½ hours

For the Artic char sashimi in a spicy broth

5 garlic cloves
20 red bird's eye chili peppers
10 oz (300 g) green onions
20 large shiitake mushrooms
2/3 cup (150 mL) light soy sauce
1 L fish stock
250 mL freshly squeezed lime juice
150 mL fish sauce
40 g sugar
200 g Arctic char fillet (sashimi quality)

For the lime gelée

200 mL freshly squeezed lime juice
10 g sugar
6 g agar flakes or powder

For the pea puree

300 g fresh peas
Salt
Ground chili peppers
1 pinch xanthan gum

Arctic char sashimi

For the spicy stock, cut the garlic into thin slices. Clean, core, and finely chop the chili peppers. Rinse the green onions and cut into rings. Clean and finely dice the mushrooms. In a medium saucepan, add the soy sauce, fish stock, lime juice, fish sauce, sugar, garlic, chili peppers, green onions, and mushrooms. Mix well and bring to a boil. After 20 minutes remove the pot from the heat and let stand for 60 minutes. Pass through a fine-mesh strainer. Before serving, pour into a decorative jug and check the fish fillet for bones and cut into slices.

Lime gelée

In a small saucepan, mix the lime juice with 1/2 cup of water, the sugar and agar powder and bring to a boil. Reduce the heat to low until the agar powder has completely dissolved, stirring constantly, about 10 minutes. Remove from the heat and allow to set well. Pour the gelée into a food processor and blend until it creates a smooth gel. Transfer to a piping bag.

Pea puree

In a medium saucepan, add the peas and plenty of water. Bring to a boil and cook until soft, about 5 minutes. Drain the peas and transfer them to a food processor. Puree until smooth, season with a little salt and chili powder and, if needed, thicken with xanthan gum. Pass the puree through a fine-mesh strainer, transfer to a piping bag and keep warm until serving.

>

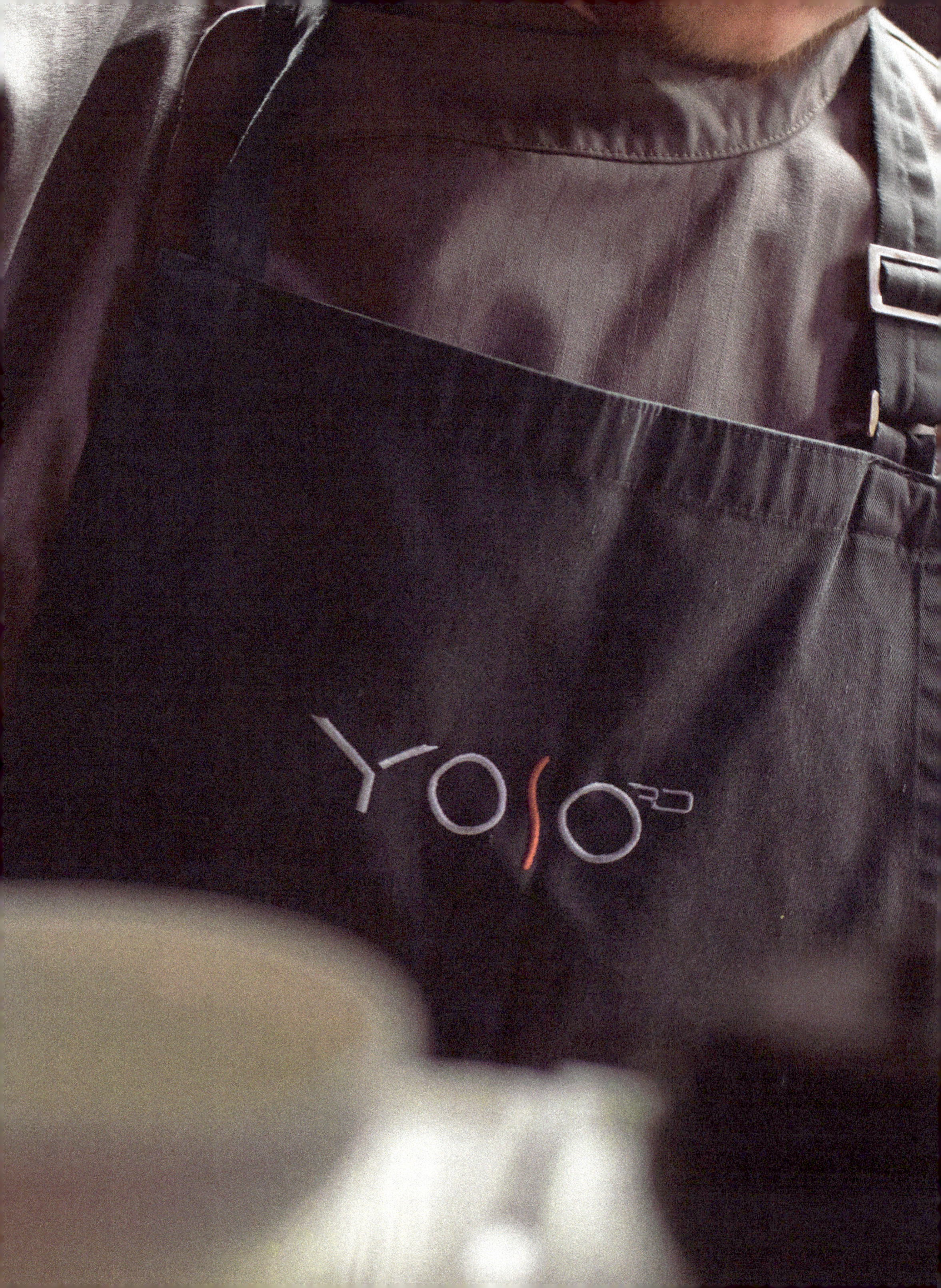
YOSO

For the vegetables
8 snow peas
5 tablespoons spicy stock
  (see previous page)
20 small shiitake
  mushrooms
2 tablespoons neutral
  vegetable oil

To serve
Pea shoots

Vegetables
Clean and trim the snow peas and julienne them diagonally. In a pan, heat the 5 tablespoons of spicy stock and add the julienned snow
peas. Clean the mushrooms. In a separate pan, heat the oil and sautée until softened.

To serve
Place three slices of Arctic char in deep plates. Place the vegetables on top and pipe a few dots of pea puree and lime gelée on top. Garnish with the pea shoots. Add the hot spicy broth at the table.

TIPS

You can also use Norwegian fjord trout or sashimi-quality salmon for this dish.

If you like very spicy dishes, keep the vegetable scraps leftover from preparing the spicy broth. Enjoy them with cooked rice in a bowl.

Hiramasa Ceviche | Daikon | Avocado

Serves 4 | Prep time: 2 hours

For the daikon rolls
250 g rice vinegar
500 g sugar
3 teaspoons ground
  turmeric
1 daikon radish

For the ceviche
1 stalk lemongrass 1 red chili
  pepper
250 mL apple juice
70 g brown sugar
35 mL rice vinegar
3 kaffir lime leaves
30 mL ponzu sauce
20 mL kalamansi puree
  (calamondin orange)
35 mL lime puree
200 g yellowfin tuna fillets

Daikon rolls
In a medium saucepan, preheat a water bath to 155°F (68°C). In a separate saucepan, add rice vinegar, sugar, turmeric, and 2 cups water (500 mL). Bring to a boil and stir until all the sugar has dissolved. Clean the radish and place in a foil bag. Fill the bag with the hot marinade and let it cool. Once cooled, vacuum seal the bag and add to the bath water. Cook for 80 minutes. Remove radish out of the vacuum bag and let drain. Using a mandolin or slicer, slice the radish lengthwise into thin slices (about 1½ x 6 cm). Then roll them up into decorative spirals.

Ceviche
Rinse the green onions, discarding the root end, and cut into thin rings. Rinse and core the chili peppers and cut into thin rings. In a medium saucepan, add the chili pepper, lemongrass, and remaining ingredients, except the fish. Bring to a boil, then remove from heat. Set the pan aside for 30 minutes to rest. Pass the mixture through a fine-mesh strainer and set aside. Cut the fish fillets into thin slices.

>

For the ponzu glaze

30 mL ponzu sauce

40 mL pear juice

50 mL soy sauce

1.8 grams agar flakes or
   powder

To serve

Avocado crème (see recipe
   for "Tuna Fish | Avocado
   | Black Radish" on page
   257)

Pickled sushi ginger, cut
   into strips

Affila cress

Mini rice pearls

Radish slices, sliced wafer
   thin

Ponzu glaze

Bring all of the ingredients to a boil in a saucepan, lower the heat and simmer for about 3 minutes, stirring constantly to ensure the agar is fully incorporated, then set aside to cool. Before serving, puree in a food processor until smooth, pour through a fine-mesh strainer and transfer to a piping bag.

To serve

Place 3 slices of fish on each plate and drizzle with the ceviche sauce. Add a few dots of ponzu glaze and avocado crème to each slice on the plate. Garnish with the daikon rolls, pickled ginger, cress shoots, mini rice pearls, and slices of radish.

TIP

If you use a Thermomix device for mixing, you should always take into account that very small quantities are difficult to process. If necessary, a larger amount (400 mlL than is actually needed for the respective dish can be prepared. The remaining glaze can then be vacuum-sealed and frozen. To make glaze, thaw the base mixture and stir until smooth with a whisk.

Coconut Lemongrass Soup | Red Shrimp | Carrots

Serves 4 | Prep time: 5 hours

For the coconut lemongrass soup

250 g assorted chicken parts (necks, legs, wings, backs)
50 g carrots
1/3 stalk of celery
150 g celeriac
100 g shallots
35 g shiitake mushrooms
35 g mushrooms
1 tablespoon neutral vegetable oil
5 coriander seeds
2 white peppercorns
50 mL fish sauce plus a little more to taste
350 mL poultry stock
1 L coconut milk
15 g red chili peppers
50 g fresh ginger
1 stalk lemongrass
15 g fresh cilantro
2 kaffir lime leaves
150 mL shellfish stock
Freshly squeezed lime juice

For the carrots

70 grams brown sugar
70 mL rice vinegar
1 ½ fresh, small red chili peppers
250 mL passion fruit juice
1 stick lemongrass
2 medium carrots

Coconut lemongrass soup

Preheat the oven to 320°F (160°C). Spread the chicken pieces on a baking sheet and roast for 60 minutes.

In the meantime, peel and finely chop the carrots, celery, celeriac, and shallots. Clean and quarter the mushrooms. Heat oil in a large saucepan over medium heat. Add the vegetables, shallots, mushrooms, and coriander seeds until soft and translucent. Then add the peppercorns. Deglaze the pan with the fish sauce and the poultry stock, scraping up the browned bits on the bottom of the pan with a wooden spoon. Reduce the liquid by half, then add the coconut milk. Reduce heat, add the roasted chicken pieces to the pan and simmer for 2 hours.

Clean the chili peppers, remove the seeds, and chop into rings. Peel the ginger and finely dice. Clean the lemongrass, then lightly smash with the back of a knife and cut into rings. Rinse and dry the cilantro and pluck the leaves. Add the chili peppers, ginger, lemongrass, cilantro leaves, kaffir lime leaves, and the shellfish stock to the soup and simmer for another 60 minutes. Finally, pass the soup through a fine-mesh strainer and pour the strained liquid back into the pot. Before serving, season the soup with the fish sauce and lime juice and serve in a decorative jug.

Carrots

Clean the chili peppers, remove the seeds, and chop into small pieces. Bring the chili peppers, sugar, rice vinegar, and passion fruit juice to a boil in a saucepan. Lower the heat and simmer for 5 minutes. Turn off the heat and let the passion fruit marinade sit for 60 minutes, then pass through a fine-mesh strainer. Peel 1 of the carrots and using a mandolin or slicer, thinly slice it lengthwise. Re-heat the passion fruit marinade, add the carrot slices and simmer for 1 minute. Remove the slices and roll into decorative spirals before serving. Peel the other carrots, cut into thick crescents. Add to the marinade and set aside.

>

6 요소 YOSO

Abfüller:

C.A. Immich-Batterieberg
Weingut GmbH & Co.KG
D 56850 Enkirch

DEUTSCHER PRÄDIKATSWEIN KABINETT

Enthält Sulfite

10.5 % Vol.

750 ml

For the filling

4 snow peas

Salt

16 small shiitake mushrooms

2 tablespoons neutral
  vegetable oil

8 raw shrimp

Filling

Clean the snow peas, cut them into thirds and blanch for
2 minutes in boiling salted water, then shock in ice water,
pass through a fine-mesh strainer and drain well. Clean the
mushrooms. Over medium-high heat, add half of the oil in a
pan and sautée until soft. Remove from pan and set aside.
Clean, devein, and peel the shrimp. In the same pan used for
mushrooms, heat the remaining oil, add the shrimp and cook 1
minute on each side.

To serve

Place the shrimp, carrot rolls, and crescents, mushrooms, and
snow peas decoratively onto a deep plate. At the table, pour the
hot coconut lemongrass soup over the filling.

Marinated Fjord Trout, Fennel Salad, & Wasabi

Serves 4 | Prep time: 1 ½ hours plus 1 day to pickle the fish

For the marinated fjord trout fillet

30 g fennel seeds, toasted
2 star anise
4 g black peppercorns
4 g whole coriander seeds
1 cardamom seed
350 g brown sugar
200 g coarse sea salt
2 stalks of lemongrass
10 g peeled ginger
Zest of 1 organic (untreated) orange
Approx. 1 kg fjord trout (with skin, enough for approx. 15 people)

For the orange glaze

100 mL orange juice
5 g vegetarian gelatin powder

Marinated fjord trout fillet

For the spice powder, toast the fennel seeds in a non-stick pan, without oil, until they are fragrant. Then put the cooled fennel seeds, star anise, peppercorns, coriander seeds, and cardamom in a food processor and mix to a fine powder. For the sugar-salt powder, mix the sugar and salt in a food processor to a fine powder. Rinse, trim the root end, and finely chop the lemongrass. Cut the peeled ginger into thin slices. For the marinade, mix 300 grams of the sugar-salt powder, 30 grams of the spice powder, lemongrass, ginger, and the grated orange peel.

Put a thin layer of the seasoning and salt mixture on a baking sheet. Place the fjord trout fillet on top with the skin side down. Spread the remaining spice and salt mixture evenly on the meat side of the fish. Make sure that the center piece of the fillet is covered with more marinade than the thinner belly flaps of the fillet. Cover the tray with cling film and place in the refrigerator. The fjord trout should remain in the marinade for 24 hours. Then remove the fjord trout from the marinade, rinse it carefully with cold water and place it on a towel to dry. Before serving, cut the trout into strips about 8-mm wide.

Orange gelée

Bring the orange juice and gelatin to a boil and simmer for 2 minutes. Pour the liquid into a square mold (about 8 x 8 cm) so that it stands about 7-mm high. Place the mold in the refrigerator to solidify the contents. Before serving, cut the gelée into cubes.

>

For the fennel salad
1/2 tablespoon fennel seeds
15 grams brown sugar
100 mL freshly pressed
  orange juice
3 grams wasabi paste
2 star anise
Juice from 1/2 a lemon
10 grams pickled sushi
  ginger
1/2 fennel bulb
1 pinch of salt

For the wasabi crème
1 teaspoon orange oil
5 teaspoons wasabi paste
1 pinch of salt
1 pinch of sugar
Zest and juice from
 1 organic (untreated)
 orange
150 grams Japanese
  mayonnaise

To serve
Fresh dill
Wasabi sesame seeds

Fennel salad
Toast the fennel seeds in a non-stick pan, without oil. In a hot pan, caramelize the brown sugar and add the fennel seeds. Deglaze with the orange juice and mix in the wasabi, star anise, and lemon juice. Bring the marinade to a boil and simmer for about 20 minutes, then pour the marinade through a fine-mesh strainer. Drain the sushi ginger, cut into fine strips, and mix with the marinade. Clean and trim the fennel and remove the stalk. Cut the fennel in half and then finely slice it in a bowl. Add the salt and mix the fennel well, then pour the marinade over the fennel.

Wasabi crème
In a saucepan, add the orange oil, wasabi paste, salt, sugar, orange zest, and orange juice, bring to a boil and then pass through a fine-mesh strainer. Before serving, mix the stock with the mayonnaise and pour into a piping bag.

To serve
Place a piece of marinated fjord trout fillet on each plate. Sprinkle a few dots of wasabi crème on top. Place several portions of rolled up fennel salad next to the fillet. Spread some orange glaze cubes around it. Finally, garnish with dill and wasabi sesame seeds.

TIPS

It's possible to freeze the marinated fjord trout. You can either portion it first, pack it in foil bags, vacuum it, and freeze it. Or you can leave it whole, wrap it in cling film, and then freeze it. If packed well, it can be stored in the refrigerator for about 2 weeks. The recipe for the marinade also goes well with fresh salmon. You can, for example, use the remaining spice mix, which can be stored in an airtight container, to create a salmon tartare. To do this, heat 1 teaspoon of spice mix in 1/2 cup (100 mL) of a neutral vegetable oil until the spices have dissolved. Pass the spicy oil through a fine-mesh strainer and use it as seasoning.

Salmon & Miso Mustard | Sashimi | Keta Caviar

Serves 4 | Prep time: 1 ½ hours

For the salmon
280 g salmon loin ("Label Rouge")

For the lime sauce
50 mL low sodium soy sauce
5 mL yuzu juice
12 mL freshly squeezed lime juice
25 mL teriyaki sauce

For the mustard and miso crème
5 g Japanese mustard powder
125 g Japanese saikyo miso paste (or light Japanese miso paste)
20 mL rice vinegar

For the tapioca
20 g tapioca
Salt
100 mL passion fruit juice
10 g mustard seeds
80 mL apple juice
80 mL passion fruit juice

To serve
Rice pearls (masago arare, available in Asian shops)
White green onion rings
Keta salmon caviar
Sorrel leaves

Salmon
Cut the salmon into thin slices (5 mm).

Lime sauce
Mix the soy sauce, yuzu juice, lime juice, teriyaki sauce, and 10 mL of water together. Before serving, transfer into a decorative jug.

Mustard and miso crème
Mix the mustard powder, 10 grams of water, soybean paste and rice vinegar to create a crème. Transfer into a piping bag.

Tapioca
Boil the tapioca in a saucepan with salted water for 3 minutes, then drain. Pour the cooked tapioca back into the pot. Pour in the passion fruit juice and cook for another 3 minutes. Remove from heat. Put the mustard seeds, apple juice, passion fruit juice, and 100 mL water in a saucepan and cook over low heat until soft. Stir occasionally, adding some water as needed. Let the mustard seeds cool, then mix with the cooked tapioca.

To serve
Place the sliced salmon in deep plates. Decorate with a few small dots of mustard and miso crème on top. Place small dollops of tapioca on the salmon using an espresso spoon. Garnish with the rice pearls, green onion rings, caviar, and sorrel leaves. At the table, pour some lime sauce over the fish.

Cashew Yin Yang

Serves 4 | Prep time: 2 hours plus 4 hours to freeze the sorbet

For the celery sorbet
Approx. 1 bunch celery
75 g sugar
60 mL freshly squeezed
  lime juice
40 g glucose
1.1 g Pectagel Rose
1 large pinch of salt

For the celery gelée
Approx. 1/3 bunch celery
4.6 g vegetarian gelatin
  powder

For the strawberry gelée
Approx. 300 g of
  strawberries
5 g vegetarian gelatin
  powder

For the cashew mousse
100 g cashew paste
150 mL coconut milk
6 sheets white gelatin
1 level teaspoon baharat
1 small pinch chili powder
1 pinch of salt
100 g egg whites
1 teaspoon sugar

Celery sorbet
Clean and trim the celery stalks, then extract the juice from the celery. You will need 350 mL of juice. Bring the juice, along with the sugar, lime juice, glucose, Pectagel Rose and salt to a boil, then transfer to a Pacojet beaker and freeze.

Celery gelée
Clean and trim the celery stalks, then extract the juice from the celery. You will need 100 mL of juice. Boil the juice together with the gelatin powder, pour it into a mold (20 x 25 cm) so that the layer is approx. 2-mm high. Let this layer set. Before serving, cut out the gelée with a "yin and yang" cookie cutter.

Strawberry gelée
Trim, clean, and juice the strawberries. You will need 100 mL of juice. Boil the juice together with the gelatin powder, pour it into a mold (20 x 25 cm) so that the layer is 2-mm high. Let this layer set. Before serving, cut out the gelée with a "yin and yang" cookie cutter.

Cashew mousse
Mix 100 mL coconut milk into the cashew paste. Soften the gelatin in cold water. Bring the rest of the coconut milk (50 mL) and the baharat, chili powder, and salt to a boil. Squeeze the liquid out of the gelatin and mix it into the spicy coconut milk. Pour the spicy coconut milk through a fine-mesh strainer into the cashew paste and stir everything together well. Beat the egg white with the sugar until stiff and carefully fold into the mixture.

Pour the cashew mousse into a mold (20 x 25 cm) so that it stands about 7-mm high. Let this layer cool for at least 4 hours. Before serving, cut out a circle with a round cookie cutter with a diameter that corresponds to the "yin and yang" cookie cutter.

For the rice vinegar gel

200 mL rice vinegar

75 g sugar

25 g salt

100 mL mirin (rice wine)

5 g agar flakes or powder

5 g kappa carrageenan

For the caramelized cashews

100 g cashews

1 level teaspoon sugar 1 pinch of salt

For the strawberry celery salad

2 stalks of celery

8 strawberries

Salt

Baharat

Freshly squeezed lime juice

Rice vinegar glaze

Bring the rice vinegar, sugar, salt, mirin, agar powder or flakes, and kappa to a boil with 100 mL of water and let cool. Pour the glaze into a food processor and mix into a smooth gel. Pass through a fine-mesh strainer, if needed.

Caramelized cashews

Put the cashew nuts in a non-stick pan and roast them without adding any fat, then roughly chop them. Put the sugar, salt, and 50 mL of water in a second pan and melt into a caramel. Add the cashews and caramelize them.

Strawberry celery salad

Clean, trim, and peel the celery. Rinse and trim the strawberries. Cut both into very fine cubes and mix in a bowl. (The percentage of celery cubes should be approx. 60 percent). Season the salad to taste with salt, baharat, and lime juice.

To serve

Place a slice of cashew mousse on each plate. Place the cut-out celery and strawberry "yin and yang" gelée pieces on top of the mousse. Form a semicircle out of caramelized cashews underneath. Place a scoop of celery sorbet in the middle. Arrange some strawberry and celery salad on each side of the sorbet. Spread small dabs of rice vinegar gel around the semicircle.

TIP

Baharat is a spice mix that originally comes from the Arab world. Similar to curry, it has no fixed composition but is produced in many regional varieties. The main ingredients are pepper (peppercorns and pods), paprika, coriander, cloves, cumin, cardamom, nutmeg, star anise, and cinnamon. It is used primarily in meat and fish dishes, but there is also, for example, coffee baharat, which is a spicy mocha.

Fried Octopus | Coriander Crumble | Mango Crème | Sweet and Sour Vegetables

Serves 4 | **Prep time:** 2 ½ hours plus 1 day to pickle the vegetables

For the coriander crumble
50 g fresh coriander
50 g panko (breadcrumbs)

For the peanut mousse
6 sheets white gelatin
150 mL coconut milk
100 g peanut paste
1 level teaspoon baharat
1 small pinch chili powder
100 g egg whites
1 pinch of salt
1 teaspoon sugar

For the sweet and sour vegetables
½ teaspoon coriander seeds
100 mL rice vinegar
500 mL apple juice
1 stalk lemongrass
2 kaffir lime leaves
10 g fresh ginger
2 sprigs of cilantro
½ teaspoon mustard seeds
1 pinch of ground tumeric
8 white asparagus stalks
8 green asparagus stalks
16 king oyster mushrooms
12 cauliflower florets

Coriander crumble
Clean and dry the cilantro and pluck the leaves. Put the leaves with the panko in a food processor and chop finely, then dry overnight in a dehydrator. Before serving, spread the cilantro crumble on a flat plate.

Peanut mousse
Soften the gelatin in cold water. Remove 2 tablespoons of the coconut milk and set aside. Mix the remaining coconut milk, peanut paste, baharat, and chili powder in a mixing bowl until creamy. Squeeze out the gelatin well, heat it up with the coconut milk that you set aside, and dissolve it. Stir the gelatin into the peanut crème. Beat the egg white with the salt and sugar until stiff and carefully fold into the peanut crème. Spread the mousse evenly on a plate about 0.5-cm high and let it set in the refrigerator. To serve, cut out two circles in different sizes. With serving rings of different diameters (around 5 cm and 7 cm), cut out two circles per plate and coat both sides with the cilantro crumble (see above).

Sweet and sour vegetables
Toast the coriander seeds in a non-stick pan, without oil. Mix together the coriander seeds, rice vinegar, apple juice, lemongrass, lime leaves, ginger, coriander, and mustard seeds, and bring to a boil in a saucepan. Let this marinade simmer for about 1 hour. Remove about half of the marinade and mix in the turmeric powder. Rinse and trim the vegetables. Peel the asparagus spears, if needed, and cut them diagonally into pieces.

Simmer half of the white asparagus spears and the cauliflower florets in the turmeric marinade for 3 minutes and leave to cool in the marinade. Simmer the green asparagus stalks, the remaining white asparagus stalks and the king oyster mushrooms in the remaining marinade for 3 minutes and let them cool in the marinade.

For the octopus

Octopus (800–1000 g)
2 L vegetable stock
2 tablespoons neutral
  vegetable oil

For the mango crème

60 g mango puree
10 g crème fraîche
Some chili oil
Salt

To serve

Affila cress
Radish, finely sliced

Octopus

Rinse the octopus under cold running water. Put the octopus in a large saucepan, pour in the vegetable stock and slowly bring it to a boil.
Cook the octopus until soft for about 1 1/2 hours, then remove the octopus from the broth and cut the tentacles into pieces about 1-cm long. Heat the oil in a pan and fry the octopus (8–10 pieces per serving) in it before serving.

Mango crème

Mix the mango puree with the crème fraîche, chili oil, and salt and pour into a squirt bottle.

To serve

Place the two slices of peanut mousse on plates with a high rim. Arrange the octopus and sweet and sour vegetables on and next to the peanut mousse. Add a few dollops of mango crème and garnish with the cress and radish slices.

TIP

You can also make larger quantities of the sweet and sour vegetables and eat them like mixed pickles. Keep them in an airtight container and stored in a cool place.

Arctic Char | King Oyster Mushrooms | Eggplant | Lime Sauce

Serves 4 | Prep time: 3 hours

For the cilantro panko crumble
1 bunch fresh cilantro
100 g panko (Asian breadcrumbs)

For the eggplant puree
2 eggplants
300 mL coconut milk
1 large pinch of salt
Some chili powder
1 pinch xanthan gum (as needed)

For the kaffir lime and coconut broth
10 g fresh ginger
1 stalk lemongrass
250 mL coconut milk
250 mL fish stock
20 mL fish sauce
10 g palm sugar
60 mL freshly squeezed lime juice
4 kaffir lime leaves
1 teaspoon cornstarch

Cilantro and panko crumble
Clean and dry the cilantro and pluck the leaves. Put the leaves with the panko in a food processor and chop finely, then dry overnight in a dehydrator. Spread the cilantro and panko crumble on a flat tray.

Eggplant puree
Peel and chop the eggplants and put them in a pot. Pour in the coconut milk so that two thirds of the eggplant pieces are covered. Cook the eggplant for about 60 minutes. Pass the contents of the pot through a fine-mesh strainer. Pour the softened eggplant into a food processor, puree, and season with salt and a little chili powder. (Xanthan gum can be added when mixing to improve the consistency.) Pass the puree through a fine-mesh strainer and transfer to a piping bag.

Kaffir lime and coconut broth
Clean and finely dice the ginger. Rinse, trim the root end, and finely chop the lemongrass. Sweat the ginger and lemongrass in a pan, then add the coconut milk, fish stock, fish sauce, sugar, and lime juice. Let the stock simmer for about 30 minutes, then add the kaffir lime leaves and simmer gently for another 15 minutes. Pass the stock through a
fine-mesh strainer and pour back into the pot. Thicken with the cornstarch mixed with 1 tablespoon of water.

For the eggplant slices

2 eggplants
30 mL kecap manis
(Indonesian sweet soy
  sauce, available in Asian
  stores)
100 mL pineapple juice

For the Asian marinade

30 g fresh cilantro
35 g Szechuan peppercorns
2 fresh red chili peppers
10 stalks of lemongrass
40 g fresh ginger, peeled
120 g sea salt
120 g brown sugar
130 mL soy sauce
100 g oyster sauce
1 tablespoon liquid honey

For the Arctic char

4 Arctic char filets (with
  skin, 150 g each)
Neutral vegetable oil for
  frying
Asian marinade (see above)
Cilantro and panko crumble
  (see above)

For the king oyster
mushrooms

10 small king oyster
  mushrooms
1 tablespoon neutral
  vegetable oil
Salt

To serve

Red oxalis
Eggplant chips

Eggplant slices

Preheat oven to 250°F (120°C). Clean and dry the eggplant, then slice into 1-cm thick slices. Heat a pan until it is smoking hot. Sear the eggplant slices on both sides and place them side by side in an ovenproof dish. Mix the kecap manis and pineapple juice and drizzle over the eggplant. Bake the eggplant for 6 minutes. Before serving, cut the slices into four quarters.

Asian marinade

Place all of the ingredients into a food processor and process into a smooth paste.

Arctic char

Preheat a water bath to 130°F (54°C). Remove the skin from the Arctic char and set aside. Cut each fillet in half lengthwise. Position the two halves on top of each other and wrap them in cling film to form a roll, then wrap the rolls tightly with aluminum foil. Cook the four rolls in the water bath for 6 minutes. Blanch the skin in hot water and clean very thoroughly, then dry in a dehydrator. Heat the oil in a saucepan to 355°F (180°C) and fry the dried char skin in it. Before serving, brush the fish fillets with the Asian marinade (see above) and then roll them in the cilantro and panko crumble.

King oyster mushrooms

Clean the king oyster mushrooms and cut them in half. Heat the oil in a saucepan, place the mushrooms in it, cut side down, and cook them. Season the mushrooms with salt.

To serve

Place each fillet in a deep plate. Arrange two eggplant quarters and a few king oyster mushrooms next to it. Place the fried fish skin on the Arctic char. Place a few dollops of eggplant puree on the plate. Roll up the oxalis leaves to form a bag and place them in the eggplant puree. Garnish with a few eggplant chips.

Fried Calamaretti | Lettuce | Celeriac

Serves 4 | Prep time: 3 hours plus 1 day to pickle the vegetables

For the pickled red onion
60 g cider vinegar
60 g sugar
1 red onion

For the salad roll dressing
70 g fresh garlic
400 g fresh ginger
100 g red chili peppers
230 g lemongrass
50 mL fish sauce
50 mL lime juice
50 g sugar

For the salad rolls
100 g peeled celeriac
Salad roll dressing (see above)
1 head of romaine lettuce
1 stalk celery
3 sprigs fresh mint
5 sprigs fresh cilantro
1/2 teaspoon red chili pepper, finely diced

Pickled red onion
Mix the cider vinegar and sugar together until the sugar is completely dissolved. Peel the onion and cut into 4-mm slices. Cover the onion slices with the marinade and seal them in a flat, airtight bowl. Let the onion slices marinate in the refrigerator for 1 day so that they turn an even pink color.

Salad roll dressing
Peel the garlic and ginger. Clean and core the chili peppers. Trim the lemongrass. Place all of the ingredients into a food processor and mix until it has reached a fine consistency, then pour into a Pacojet beaker. Pacotize the spice paste at least twice so that the paste has a very fine consistency. (You can also pass the paste through a fine-mesh strainer.) You will need 50 grams of the paste. Mix the fish sauce, lime juice, and sugar with 50 mL of water in a bowl until the sugar has completely dissolved. Mix the dressing (200 mL) with 50 grams of the spice paste.

Salad rolls
Using a slicer, cut the celeriac into very thin slices. Heat the dressing (see above) in a saucepan and bring the celeriac to a boil for 30 seconds. Remove from stove and let cool. Clean the lettuce, remove the stalk, and cut into fine strips. Remove the long threads from the celery stalk and then cut into thin julienne strips about 4-cm long. Put the lettuce and celery strips in a bowl. Clean and dry the herbs and pluck the leaves, then finely chiffonade the leaves and add to the salad. Add the finely diced chili pepper to the salad. Remove the celeriac slices from the dressing and let it drain well. Pour the dressing over the salad and mix everything well. Spread the celeriac slices out on the work surface, arrange the julienned and chiffonaded herbs on top and roll the celeriac slice into a roll. Before serving, cut the roll into thirds.

>

For the cilantro puree
2 bunches fresh cilantro
Approx. 700 g of celeriac
250 mL coconut milk
Salt
1 pinch xanthan gum

For the calamaretti (squid)
12 squid tubes (each about
  70–100 g, fresh or frozen)
2 tablespoons olive oil
Salt
Freshly squeezed lime juice
Chili oil (if desired)

Cilantro puree
Preheat a steam cooker (100 percent steam) to 390°F (200°C). Clean and dry the cilantro and pluck the leaves. Blanch the leaves in hot water and shock them in an ice water bath. Wrap the cilantro in a cloth and squeeze thoroughly so that as much water is removed as possible. Transfer the leaves to a Pacojet beaker and freeze. Pacotize the cilantro at least twice in the Pacojet so that the paste (cilantro) has a very fine consistency. Peel and dice the celeriac. Put 500 grams of celeriac cubes and the coconut milk in a foil bag,

Calamaretti (squid)
Gently twist and pull to remove the head and viscera from the body, make an incision behind the eye, push the mouth a little to the side and cut off the edible head, discarding the viscera. Remove the "backbone" (cuttlebone). Thoroughly rinse the body and tentacles and remove the skin. Slice the tubes open (butterfly) and carefully cut the inside into a diamond shape, being careful not to cut the meat all the way through. Heat the oil in a pan and fry the calamaretti (head and tubes) briefly. (Be careful: If the calamaretti is fried too long, it will turn rubbery!) Season to taste with a little salt and lime juice. If you like it spicy, you can also add a few drops of chili oil.

1 leek
Neutral vegetable oil for
  frying
Salt

To serve
Pickled red onion

Fried leeks
Clean, drain, and trim the leek. Cut the white of the leek into fine strips. Heat the oil to 340°F (170°C). Fry the leek strips in the oil, carefully remove, and drain on kitchen paper. Season with a pinch of salt.

To serve
Place a salad roll upright in each of the preheated bowls. Arrange the calamaretti tubes and heads next to it. Add a few dollops of cilantro puree and drizzle with the dressing. Garnish with the fried leek and some pickled red onion.

TIPS

If there's any spice paste leftover, you can divide it into rolls, wrap it in cling film, and store it in the freezer. You can also use it to season a coconut soup or sauce. The more cilantro you use to make the cilantro paste, the better. That's because the Pacojet's knives know how to attack its tiny surfaces.

Zander | Broccolini | Banana-Curry Sauce

Serves 4 | Prep time: 2 ½ hours plus 1 day to pickle the vegetables

For the pickled cauliflower
50 g Japanese rice vinegar
  for sushi (e.g., Mizkan)
100 g sugar
1 teaspoon ground turmeric
8 cauliflower florets

For the cauliflower puree
300 g cauliflower
200 mL coconut milk
Chili powder
1 squeeze of lime juice
1 pinch xanthan gum

For the broccolini
40 mL rice vinegar
40 g sugar
100 g broccolini florets

For the yellow curry paste
125 g dried red chili peppers
Salt
30 g fresh garlic
5 g black peppercorns
10 g salt
30 g galangal
30 g fresh ginger, peeled
100 g lemongrass
10 g kaffir lime leaves
50 g fresh cilantro
100 g shallots
1 star anise
2 cinnamon sticks
5 g coriander seeds
50 mL toasted sesame oil
100 mL corn oil
10 g hot paprika powder
10 g ground turmeric

Pickled cauliflower
Bring the rice vinegar, sugar, and turmeric to a boil with 50 mL of water. Preheat a water bath to 155°F (68°C). Put the cauliflower florets in a foil bag, pour the hot stock over them, vacuum seal the bag, and cook for 2 hours in the water bath.

Cauliflower puree
Preheat a steam cooker (100 percent steam) to 390°F (100°C). Clean and chop the cauliflower. Put the cauliflower and coconut milk in a foil bag, vacuum seal and cook in the steam cooker for about 60 minutes. Pour the contents of the vacuum bag into a food processor and blend into a fine puree. Season with a little chili powder and lime juice and thicken with xanthan gum.

Broccolini topping
Mix the vinegar and sugar well. Place the broccolini florets with the vinegar and sugar solution in a foil bag and vacuum seal. Marinate for 1 hour.

Yellow curry paste
Remove the seeds from the chili peppers for the curry paste, then soak the chili peppers in salted water for 30 minutes. Drain the chili peppers well, put the remaining ingredients in a food processor and puree
until fine.

For the banana-curry sauce

1 tablespoon neutral
 vegetable oil
50 g yellow curry paste (see
 above)
50 g lemongrass
1 tablespoon ground
 turmeric
3 kaffir lime leaves
1 ripe banana
500 mL coconut milk

For the fish

2 tablespoons neutral
 vegetable oil
4 zander filets (perch, pike
 or walleye, with skin, 120 g
 each)
Salt

For the broccolini

100 mL mango juice
16 broccolini florets

Banana-curry sauce

Heat the oil in a pan. Cook the curry paste in it until it starts to become fragrant. Press the lemongrass down a little with the back of a knife, then stir it into the turmeric, lime leaves, crushed banana, and coconut milk. Let the curry sauce simmer for a few minutes, then transfer the sauce to a food processor and puree finely. Before serving, pass it through a fine-mesh strainer again.

Zander

Heat the oil in a pan. Cook the fish, skin-side down, for 3 minutes, then turn the fillets, and cook them briefly on the meat side. Season with a pinch of salt.

Broccolini

Heat up the mango juice and cook the broccolini florets in it for 2 minutes..

To serve

Spread some cauliflower puree artfully on deep plates and add a small circle of the banana-curry sauce. Place a fish fillet on top and arrange the cauliflower and broccolini florets around the outside. Garnish with the broccolini.

TIP

You can easily prepare and freeze the yellow curry paste in individual portions by putting some in an ice cube tray. Take out a cube or two whenever you need some.

Codfish | Lentils | Blood Orange | Peanuts

Serves 4 | Prep time: 2 ½ hours

For the blood orange jelly
100 g blood orange juice
5 g vegetarian gelatin
  powder

For the peanut sauce
80 g peanuts
50 g shallots
1 tablespoon neutral
  vegetable oil
300 mL fish stock
100 mL coconut milk Salt
Ground chili peppers

For the lentils
20 g diced shallots
15 g green onions, finely
  chopped
2 g dried curry leaves
Salt
1 tablespoon neutral
  vegetable oil
50 g dry
beluga lentils
1 red chili pepper
10 g carrots, finely diced
Some soy sauce

For the cod
4 cod filets (with skin, 120 g
  each)
Salt

To serve
Caramelized peanuts
Red Oxalis
Daikon cress

Blood orange jelly
Mix the juice and gelatin in a saucepan, bring to a boil and let simmer for 2 minutes. Pour the liquid into a square mold (8 x 8 cm) so that it stands about 4-mm high. Cool the mold to set the jelly. Before serving, cut out circles 1 cm in diameter with a cookie cutter.

Peanut sauce
Toast the peanuts in a non-stick pan, without oil. Peel and finely slice the shallots. Heat the oil in a pan and sauté the shallots in it. Add the roasted peanuts. Add the fish stock and coconut milk and season with salt and a little chili powder. Let the sauce simmer for a few minutes, then transfer it to a food processor or blender and puree until fine. Pass the sauce through a fine-mesh strainer.

Lentils
In a saucepan, mix together the diced shallot, 10 grams of green onions, curry leaves, a little salt, and 200 mL of water, bring to a boil and then strain through a fine-mesh strainer. Heat the oil in a pan and sauté the lentils in it. Gradually add in the stock and let it keep boiling until the lentils are soft. Clean the chili peppers, remove the seeds, and dice very finely. After about 15 minutes, add the diced chili peppers and carrots to the lentils and simmer for another 5 minutes until the lentils are soft. Season with soy sauce to taste.

Cod
Put the cod in very little water in a pan, put on the lid and steam for 8 minutes until soft. Season with a pinch of salt.

To serve
Arrange the lentils in a semicircle on deep plates and pour in some peanut sauce. Place a cod fillet on top of each plate. Place two blood orange jelly circles next to it. Garnish with the caramelized peanuts, oxalis leaves, and cress.

Tuna | Avocado | Black Radish

Serves 4 | Prep time: 2 hours plus 36 hours to marinate the tuna

For the tuna
5 g cardamom seeds
5 g star anise
50 g raw cane sugar
5 g coarse sea salt
2 g white peppercorns
10 g red chili peppers
40 g green onions
10 g fresh cilantro
160 g toasted sesame oil
30 g oyster sauce
60 mL soy sauce
40 mL corn oil
1 kg tuna steaks

For the black radish
50 mL apple juice
15 g brown sugar
45 mL rice vinegar
1 stalk lemongrass
1 kaffir lime leaf
10 mL ponzu sauce
1 black radish
2 g squid ink

Tuna
For the tuna marinade, put the cardamom, star anise, sugar, salt and peppercorns in a food processor or grinder and mix to a fine spice powder. Remove the seeds from the chili pepper, and finely chop. Rinse the green onions and cut into thin rings. Clean and dry the cilantro and pluck the leaves. Finely chop the leaves. In bowl, mix the chili pepper, green onion, and coriander with the sesame oil, oyster sauce, soy sauce, and corn oil, then stir in the spice powder. Remove 4 tablespoons and set aside. Cut the tuna steaks into a rectangle (7 x 10 x 8 cm) and set the extra pieces aside. Place the cut tuna and the remaining marinade in a foil bag, vacuum seal, and marinate in the refrigerator for 36 hours. Turn the vacuum bag over twice during the 36 hours. Remove the tuna from the bag, clean it carefully, and pat dry. Before serving, cut the tuna into 4-mm thin slices.

Black Radish
Mix the apple juice, sugar, rice vinegar, finely chopped lemongrass, lime leaf, and ponzu sauce together well. Clean and dry the radish and, using a slicer, cut into 1-mm thin slices. Pour half of the marinade with half of the radish slices in a foil bag and vacuum seal it. Dye the remaining marinade black with the sepia ink, then pour into a foil bag with the remaining radish slices and vacuum seal. Let the two different radish preparations marinate in the refrigerator for 36 hours. Before serving, remove radish slices from the vacuum bag and drain.

\>

For the tuna crème
200 g reserved tuna cuts
 (see "Tuna" above)
80 mL coconut milk
Soy sauce
Chili powder

For the sepia chips
1 g salt
5 g squid ink
10 g butter
10 g tempura flour
25 g powdered sugar
30 g egg whites

For the tuna tartare filling
100 g raw tuna (sashimi
 quality)
1 ripe avocado
1 daikon radish
Some togarashi seasoning
 mix
1 squeeze of lime juice
Salt

Tuna crème
Preheat a water bath to 133°F (56°C). Put the extra cuts of fish in a foil bag, vacuum seal and cook in the water bath for 60 minutes. Transfer the fish to a food processor or blender and puree it with the coconut milk, some soy sauce, and some chili powder. Pour the crème through a fine-mesh strainer and then transfer to a piping bag.

Sepia chips
Preheat oven to 320°F (160°C). Bring 100 mL of water, the salt, sepia ink, and butter to a boil in a saucepan. Mix the tempura flour, powdered sugar, and egg white together in a mixing bowl, then gradually stir in the slightly cooled sepia water. Spread this dough thinly on a silicone baking mat and bake for 15 minutes. Remove from the oven. Cut circles out of the dough with a round cookie or biscuit cutter (3.5 cm in diameter). Put the sheet back in the oven and bake the circles for another 15 minutes. Allow the circles to cool and seal them in a vacuum bag.

Tuna tartare filling
Cut the raw tuna into very small cubes. Cut the avocado in half, remove the pit and then remove the pulp with a spoon. Finely chop the avocado into very small cubes. Peel and finely chop the radish. Mix the chopped ingredients in a bowl and season with togarashi spice mixture, lime juice, and salt. Spread the tuna slices on the worktop and place a length of filling on them. Roll up the tuna and coat the outside with the tuna marinade that you set aside.

For the avocado crème
1 ripe avocado
Salt
1 squeeze of lime juice
Some chili powder

To serve
Cubes of yellow daikon (see
  "Hiramas Ceviche | Daikon
  | Avocado" on p. 214, but
  chop the daikon into cubes
  instead of spirals)
Mini sorrel leaves
Yuzu sesame seeds

Avocado crème
Cut the avocado in half, remove the pit and then remove the pulp with a spoon. In a blender, finely puree the pulp and season with salt, lime juice, and chili powder. Strain the crème through a fine-mesh strainer and then transfer to a piping bag.

To serve
Place a stuffed tuna roll on each plate and place two sepia chips on the ends. Arrange a few dollops of tuna crème, avocado crème, and yellow daikon cubes on the plate. Roll the white and black radish slices up into a spiral and place them upright on the plate. Garnish with the sorrel leaves and yuzu sesame seeds.

TIP

Shichimi togarashi is a spice mixture from Japan, whose name means "seven-flavor chili pepper" in reference to its blend of seven ingredients. Outside of Japan it is also known as nanami togarashi. The spice blend consists of roasted mandarin or orange peel (chenpi), black and white sesame seeds, poppy seeds, hemp seeds, nori or anori and coarsely ground Szechuan pepper. Ichimi togarashi is a ground chili pepper.

Black Feathered Chicken | Chicory | Red Curry

Serves 4 | Prep time: **3 ½ hours**

For the ponzu gelée
80 mL ponzu sauce
30 g sugar
5 g vegetarian gelatin
  powder

For the Jerusalem artichoke
  puree
500 g Jerusalem artichokes
300 mL coconut milk
Chili powder
Salt
1 pinch xanthan gum for
  binding (as desired)

For the black feathered
  chicken
400 g black feathered
  chicken breast (with skin)
2 tablespoons toasted
  sesame oil
1 tablespoon neutral
  vegetable oil

For the chicory
1 tablespoon fennel seeds
20 g brown sugar
125 mL freshly squeezed
  orange juice
60 mL passion fruit juice
1 star anise
5 g wasabi paste
1 pinch of chili powder
4 mini chicories
100 g cooked edamame

Ponzu gelée
Mix the ponzu sauce, sugar, and gelatin powder and bring to a boil, then pour it into a small, square serving mold (4 x 4 cm) so that the liquid is about 7-mm high. Let the liquid cool. Before serving, cut the gelée into cubes.

Jerusalem artichoke puree
Preheat a steam cooker (100 percent steam) to 215°F (100°C). Peel the Jerusalem artichoke and cut into walnut-sized pieces. Put the pieces, along with the coconut milk, in a foil bag, vacuum seal and cook for about 70 minutes.

Pour the contents of the vacuum bag into a food processor and blend into a fine puree. Season the puree with chili powder and salt. Bind with the xanthan gum as desired. Before serving, transfer the puree into a piping bag.

Black feathered chicken
Preheat a steam cooker (100 percent steam) to 135°F (56°C). Put the chicken and sesame oil in a foil bag, vacuum seal and cook in the steam cooker for about 23 minutes. Remove the chicken from the bag and let it drain well. Heat the oil in a pan. Cook the meat, skin side down, until crispy, then turn and cook briefly on the meat side.

For the chicory
In a non-stick pan, toast the fennel seeds, without oil. Set aside. Heat a separate pan, caramelize the sugar in it. Add the roasted fennel seeds and deglaze with the orange juice and passion fruit juice. Stir in the star anise, wasabi paste and chili powder. Trim the heads of chicory and cut in half. Place the halved chicory in a foil bag and fill up to a third with the stock. Vacuum seal the bag and cook in a steam cooker preheated to 215°F (100°C) at 100 percent steam for 12 minutes. Then let the vacuum bag cool down in ice water. Before serving, pour the contents of the vacuum bag into a sauté pan and heat them together with the edamame.

>

For the red curry

125 g dried red
chili peppers
Salt
30 g peeled garlic
30 g fresh ginger, peeled
100 g lemongrass, trimmed
100 g shallots, peeled
5 g fresh ground black
  pepper
30 g galangal
10 g kaffir lime leaves plus 3
  extra leaves
50 g fresh cilantro
1 star anise
2 cinnamon sticks
5 g coriander seeds
50 mL toasted sesame oil
100 mL corn oil
10 g hot paprika powder
5 g red pepper flakes
200 mL poultry stock
400 mL coconut milk
Approx. 15 mL fish sauce
2 pinches of palm sugar
2 stalks of lemongrass

For the Jerusalem artichoke
  chips

1 Jerusalem artichoke tuber
Neutral vegetable oil for
  frying
Salt

To serve

Daikon cress

Red curry

To make the red curry paste, remove the seeds from the chili peppers and soak in salted water, then pour through a fine-mesh strainer, and drain well. Put the chili peppers, garlic, ginger, lemongrass, shallots, pepper, 10 grams of salt, galangal, 10 grams of lime leaves, coriander, star anise, cinnamon sticks, coriander seeds, sesame oil, corn oil, paprika powder, and red pepper flakes in a food processor or blender and blend into a fine paste. Sweat 40 grams of this red chili paste in a saucepan and add the chicken stock and coconut milk. Mix in the fish sauce, palm sugar, lemongrass, remaining lime leaves and a little salt. Let the red curry simmer for a few minutes.

Jerusalem artichoke chips

Using a slicer, cut the unpeeled Jerusalem artichoke into thin slices. Heat the oil in a saucepan to 355°F (180°C) and cook the slices until they are golden brown. Drain the chips on paper towels and season with salt.

To serve

Use two halves of the chicory to form an arch on preheated, flat plates. Arrange the edamame, two ponzu gelée cubes and a few dollops of Jerusalem artichoke puree around it. Garnish with the Jerusalem artichoke chips and cress. Pour the red curry onto the plate in the shape of a figure eight and place two slices of black feathered chicken on top of it.

TIP

You can easily prepare and store the red curry paste in individual portions. Just put some into ice cube trays. When you need a bit of paste, simply remove a cube or two from the freezer.

Short Ribs | Pumpkin | Bok Choy

Serves 4 | Prep time: 3 hours

For the short ribs

1 Spanish onion
2 carrots
1 leek
1/2 bulb of garlic
1 red chili pepper
60 g fresh ginger
2 stalks of lemongrass
4 tablespoon neutral
  vegetable oil
60 g tomato paste
150 mL light soy sauce
1 L pear juice
100 mL toasted sesame oil
10 g hot paprika powder
2 kg of short ribs (mid-rib,
  with bones)
Cornstarch

For the pumpkin puree

1 muscat pumpkin
80 mL mango juice
30 mL rice vinegar
70 mL passion fruit juice
1/2 teaspoon liquid honey
Salt
Some gochugaru (Korean
  chili flakes

Short ribs

Peel the onion, peel the carrots, and trim the leek. Finely chop the vegetables into very small cubes. Peel the garlic, clean the chili pepper, and remove the seeds. Peel the ginger and clean the lemongrass, then finely chop everything. Preheat oven to 285°F (140°C). Heat half of the vegetable oil (2 tbsp) in a pan. Sauté the onion, carrots, and leek in it. Add the tomato paste and heat briefly, then add the garlic, chili pepper, ginger, and lemongrass and sauté. Pour the soy sauce, pear juice, and sesame oil over it and season with the paprika powder. Transfer the vegetables into a lockable roaster. Heat the remaining oil (2 tbsp) in a separate pan and sear the meat on all sides, then place the meat on top of the vegetables in the roaster. The meat should be about three-quarters covered with liquid. If needed, add a little more water. Braise the meat in the closed roaster for 60 minutes, then flip the meat and simmer for another 60 minutes in the closed pot. (Cooking test: The meat should separate from the bone very easily.) Remove the meat from the sauce to cool. Transfer the sauce to a saucepan, reduce it to taste and bind with the cornstarch. Cut up the meat into portions and heat it in the sauce.

Pumpkin puree

Preheat the oven to 355°F (180°C). Clean, dry, and quarter the pumpkin. Remove the pumpkin seeds, wrap the pumpkin quarters in parchment paper and place on a baking sheet. Bake the pumpkin for about 90 minutes. Let the pumpkin cool down, then lift the pulp out of the skin. You will need 400 grams of cooked pumpkin. Mix the cooked pumpkin with the mango juice, rice vinegar, passion fruit juice, honey, a little salt and chili flakes in a food process or blender to a fine puree. Strain the puree through a fine-mesh strainer, transfer to a piping bag, and keep warm until serving.

>

요소

YOSO

For the caramelized pumpkin seeds

50 g pumpkin seeds
50 g powdered sugar
1 pinch of Maldon sea salt flakes

For the sweet and sour pumpkin

1/4 red kuri squash
300 mL apple juice
50 g sugar
100 mL rice vinegar
10 mL soy sauce
1 teaspoon finely chopped chili pepper
1/2 stalk lemongrass

For the julienne pumpkin

100 g Muscat pumpkins
30 mL rice vinegar
30 g sugar
1 pinch of salt

For the bok choy

4 bok choy leaves
4 tablespoons mango juice

To serve

Nasturtium

Caramelized pumpkin seeds

Roast the pumpkin seeds in a stainless-steel pan and dust with the powdered sugar. Let the sugar caramelize and season with the Maldon sea salt. Next, spread the caramel on a piece of baking paper and, after it cools, cut it into small pieces.

Sweet and sour pumpkin

Cut the pumpkin into six parts. Dissolve the sugar in the apple juice and add the rice vinegar, soy sauce, chili pepper, and lemongrass. Bring the stock to a boil and cook the pumpkin wedges in it until soft, then set the pan aside to soak.

Julienne pumpkin

Peel the pumpkin and, using a slicer, cut into 2-mm thin slices. From the slices, cut fine julienne strips. Dissolve the sugar in the rice vinegar and season to taste with salt. Marinate the julienned pumpkin in it.

Bok choy

Clean, trim, and dry the bok choy leaves with the white stalk. Bring to a boil together with the mango juice and then set aside.

To serve

Place a short rib on each of the preheated plates. Arrange a few dollops of pumpkin puree, a few pieces of sweet and sour pumpkin, and the bok choy along the outside. Arrange the julienne pumpkin and the caramelized pumpkin seeds on the meat. Garnish with the nasturtium.

Chocolate | Yogurt | Physalis

Serves 4 | Prep time: 2 ½ hours plus 1 day to freeze the frozen yogurt and the sphere

For the yogurt and calamansi ice cream
250 g yogurt (3.5% milk fat)
35 g powdered sugar
60 g quark (low-fat)
25 g cream
25 g whole milk
Zest and juice from
1 organic (untreated)
  orange
60 g calamansi puree
  (calamondin orange)
10 g dehydrated glucose

For the passion fuit sphere
25 grams calamansi
  puree
25 g calamansi puree
  (calamondin orange)
130 g passion fruit puree
35 g brown sugar
1 kaffir lime leaf
1/2 stalk lemongrass
30 g physalis
  (groundcherries or Cape
  gooseberries)
1 pinch xanthan gum
160 g passion fruit puree
10 g vegetarian
gelatin powder

For the yogurt and chocolate bars
2 ½ sheets of white gelatin
240 g couverture chocolate
  (>60% cocoa solids)
150 mL whole milk
45 g egg yolks
85 g sugar
15 g cocoa powder   >
220 g cream

Yogurt and calamansi ice cream
In a saucepan, mix all of the ingredients and bring to a boil, then transfer to a Pacojet beaker. Freeze the beaker. Before serving, pacotize the ice cream. (Alternatively, prepare the ice cream in an ice cream maker according to the instructions or pour the ice cream base into a mold and freeze it in the freezer. Stir vigorously several times during the first few hours. Just before serving, remove the ice cream from the freezer and let it thaw a little.)

Passion fruit sphere
Bring the Kalamansi fruit puree, passion fruit puree, sugar, lime leaf, lemongrass, and physalis to a boil and thicken slightly with a little xanthan gum. Pass the puree through a fine-mesh strainer and pour into semispherical molds (2 cm in diameter). Freeze the molds. Bring the passion fruit juice and gelatin to a boil, then let cool. Before serving, dip the frozen semicircles in the glaze.

Yogurt and chocolate bars
For the chocolate crème, soak 1 1/2 sheets of gelatin in cold water. Roughly chop 120 grams of the couverture chocolate and melt it together with the milk over a water bath. Squeeze out the gelatin and dissolve it in the milk mixture. In a mixing bowl, beat the egg yolks with 60 grams of sugar and the cocoa powder and stir in the milk mixture at room temperature. Whip 120 grams of cream until stiff and fold in. Pour this chocolate crème into a square mold and freeze.

For the crispy base, roughly chop the remaining couverture (120 grams), melt it with the cocoa butter over a warm water bath and let it cool to about 90°F (30°C). Mix the cookie crumbs with the warm chocolate. Pour this mixture onto a baking sheet covered with parchment paper and cover with another sheet of parchment paper. Roll out the mixture thinly with a rolling pin and place the tray in the refrigerator.

For the yogurt glaze, bring the yogurt to a boil until it is completely flocculated. Pour the mixture through a fine-mesh

>

35 g cocoa butter
100 g cookie crumbs
500 g yogurt (3.5% milk fat)
About 100 mL cream
1 g agar flakes or powder

For the yogurt gel
About 800 g yogurt (3.5%
  milk fat)
100 g cream
50 g sugar
1 pinch of salt
1 g gellan gum
5 g agar flakes or powder
20 g calamansi puree
  (calamondin orange)

For the chocolate tuile
50 g egg whites
35 g powdered sugar
10 g cocoa powder
20 g wheat starch

For the passion fruit tuile
120 g passion fruit puree
100 g sugar
60 g cake flour
60 g butter

strainer and collect the clear liquid. Add the rest of the cream to the clear liquid until it reaches a total weight of 250 grams. Soften the rest of the gelatin (1 sheet) in cold water. Put the cream mixture in a saucepan and bring to a boil with the remaining sugar (25 grams) and agar flakes or powder. Squeeze out the gelatin, dissolve it in a little of the hot cream mixture and then stir into the rest of the cream mixture.

To finish the yoghurt chocolate bars, cut out the crispy base and chocolate crème with a rectangular mold. Place the base as the first layer in the mold and put the chocolate crème on top. Finish by pouring the yogurt glaze over it. To set, chill the bars in the refrigerator.

Yogurt gel
Bring the yogurt to a boil until it is completely flocculated. Pour the mixture through a fine-mesh strainer and collect the clear liquid. Remove 400 mL of the clear liquid and mix with the cream, sugar, and salt. Add the gellan and agar flakes or powder to the mixture and bring to a boil. Stir in the kalamansi fruit puree and then chill to set. Pour the mixture into a food processor and process into a smooth gel. Pass the puree through a fine-mesh strainer and transfer to a piping bag.

Chocolate tuile
Preheat the oven to 360°F (180°C). Mix all ingredients and spread them onto a baking sheet with a brush. Bake the tuiles for 5 minutes. Immediately bend the baked tuiles into the desired shape and allow to cool. Store in an airtight container.

For the passion fruit chili pepper stock

100 g brown sugar
250 g passion fruit juice
100 g rice vinegar
1 chili pepper
1 stick lemongrass
2 kaffir lime leaves
50 g passion fruit puree
1 g agar flakes or powder
0.5 g gellan gum

For the physalis compote

1 tablespoon brown sugar
1 shot of dry white wine
200 mL passion fruit
chili pepper stock (see partial recipe)
1 pinch xanthan gum
2 physalis (groundcherries or Cape gooseberries)

To serve

Quinoa
Red oxalis

Passion fruit tuile

Preheat the oven to 260°F (130°C) Mix all ingredients until they form a smooth batter. Using a round stencil, spread a thin layer of the batter across a silicone baking mat and bake for about 30 minutes.

Passion fruit chili pepper stock

Bring the sugar, passion fruit juice, rice vinegar, chili pepper, lemongrass, lime leaves, and fruit pulp to a boil. Let stand for 30 minutes and then pass through a fine-mesh strainer. For the passion fruit chili gel, remove ½ cup (100 mL) of the stock, bring to a boil with the agar flakes or powder and gellan and refrigerate to set. Before serving, blend the gel in a food processor and pour into a piping bag.

Physalis compote

In a hot pan, caramelize the sugar and deglaze with the white wine. Pour in the passion fruit and chili stock and cook until the caramelized sugar has dissolved. Bind the stock with xanthan gum. Rinse, trim, dry, and cut the physalis in halves or quarters. Put the fruit in a screw-top jar, pour the hot stock over it and hermetically seal the jar. Let the compote sit for at least 1 day. It can be kept hermetically sealed for a few weeks.

To serve

Place the yogurt and chocolate bars in the middle of the plate. Place a scoop of yogurt and calamansi ice cream on top of a few grains of quinoa. Place a passion fruit sphere on top of the bars. Spread the physalis compote on and next to the bars. Add a few small dots of passion fruit chili gel and yogurt gel. In an upright position, gently insert the passion fruit tuile into the bars to fix it in place. Garnish with two chocolate tuiles and two oxalis leaves.

Raspberries | Rhubarb

Serves 4 | Prep time: 2 ½ hours plus 1 day to freeze the sorbet and to cool the ganache

For the preserved rhubarb
600 g rhubarb
100 g sugar
100 mL dry white wine
200 mL rhubarb juice
85 g raspberry puree

For the raspberry sorbet
250 g raspberry puree
70 g sugar
5 g lemon juice
5 g glucose powder

For the kaffir lime ganache
75 g white chocolate
 couverture
125 g cream
2 kaffir lime leaves

For the raspberry meringue
30 g egg whites
50 g sugar
½ teaspoon fruit powder
 "black currant"
15 g raspberry puree
15 grams raspberry puree

Preserved rhubarb
Clean, peel, and cut the rhubarb into pieces. In a saucepan, caramelize the sugar and deglaze with the white wine and rhubarb juice. Then stir in the raspberry puree. Simmer the stock until all of the caramel has dissolved. Put the rhubarb pieces together with the hot caramel stock in a foil bag, vacuum seal and marinate for 1 day.

Raspberry sorbet
Boil the raspberry puree with ½ cup (100 mL) of water, the sugar, lemon juice, and glucose powder. Transfer to a Pacojet beaker and freeze. Before serving, divide into four portions in the Pacojet. (Alternatively, prepare the sorbet in an ice cream maker according to the instructions or pour the sorbet base into a mold and put in the freezer. During the first few hours, stir vigorously several times. Just before serving, remove the sorbet from the freezer and let it thaw a little.)

Kaffir lime ganache
Roughly chop the couverture. Bring the cream with kaffir lime leaves to a boil, pour the mix over the couverture and dissolve it completely while stirring. Chill the chocolate and cream mixture for 12 hours. Then remove the lime leaves, whip the cream with a hand mixer until stiff and pour into a piping bag.

Raspberry meringue
Beat the egg whites in a food processor until stiff, gradually drizzling in the sugar. Do the same with the fruit powder and raspberry puree. Pour the meringue into a piping bag and squirt dots of meringue on a baking sheet. Dry the raspberry meringue overnight in a dehydrator. (You can also dry the meringue in an oven preheated to 210°F (100°C) with the oven door open a crack for 150 minutes. Then switch off the oven and, with the oven door slightly open, continue drying the meringue overnight using the residual heat.)

>

For the rice crème

475 g coconut milk

1 pinch of salt

2 sheets of gelatin (one package or 1 tablespoon of powdered gelatin equals 4 sheets)

100 g round grain rice

30 g sugar

90 g white chocolate couverture

90 g cream

Juice from 1/2 a lime

For the kaffir lime foam

1 sheet gelatin

250 g coconut milk

Juice from 1 lime

3 kaffir lime leaves

25 g sugar

For the coconut crumble

50 g coconut flakes

50 g sugar

50 g cake flour

5 g butter

To serve

Green oxalis

Fresh raspberries

Rice crème

Combine 1 ¼ cups (300 g) coconut milk with ½ cup (100 mL) water and the salt. Add the rice and let it steep for about 30 minutes at a low temperature. Soften ½ sheet gelatin in cold water, then squeeze the water out. Just before the end of the 30-minutes cooking time, stir in the sugar and gelatin sheets. Then set the rice aside. Soak the remaining gelatin (1 ½ sheets) in cold water, then squeeze the water out. Roughly chop the couverture. Bring the cream to a boil, pour it over the couverture and dissolve it completely while stirring. Stir the remaining gelatin into the melted chocolate. Mix in the remaining coconut milk and lime juice. Stir the chocolate crème into the rice. Pour the rice crème into round molds and refrigerate

Kaffir lime foam

Soften the gelatin in cold water. Bring the coconut milk, lime juice, lime leaves, and sugar to a boil. Squeeze the liquid out of the gelatin and mix it into the coconut milk. Let the mixture steep for 20 minutes, then pass it through a fine-mesh strainer and pour it into a siphon bottle and screw on a capsule (if needed, 2 capsules). Chill the bottle for at least 4 hours.

Coconut crumble

Preheat the oven to 320°F (160°C). Knead all of the ingredients and crumble on a baking sheet. Bake the crumble in the preheated oven for 20-30 minutes until golden brown.

To serve

Put the rice crème on plates. Arrange some preserved rhubarb pieces around it. Place a large dollop of kaffir lime foam and two small dollops of kaffir lime ganache next to the crème. Spread the coconut crumble and two raspberry meringues around the plate and place a small scoop of raspberry sorbet on the crème. Garnish with the oxalis leaves and fresh raspberries.

"Yoso-Style" Carrot Cake

Serves 4 | Prep time: 2 ½ hours plus 1 day to freeze the ice cream

For the pandan ice cream
100 g pandan leaves
500 mL coconut milk
2 g Pectagel Rose
85 g brown sugar
10 g liquid honey
170 g egg yolks
3 g salt

For the carrot cake
1 egg
150 g sugar
150 g cake flour
60 g ground almonds
1 teaspoon baking powder
150 g corn oil
225 g grated carrots
20 g grated fresh ginger

For the carrot and vanilla puree
250 g carrots
Salt
15 g sugar plus a little more to taste
1/2 vanilla bean
7 g lemon juice
1 xanthan gum

Pandan ice cream
Cut the pandan leaves into small pieces. Bring them to a boil in the coconut milk, then set aside for 20 minutes to allow them to steep. Pass the flavored coconut milk through a fine-mesh strainer into a mixing bowl. Mix the Pectagel Rose with the sugar and mix into the coconut milk and add honey, egg yolk, and salt. Emulsify the mixture over a warm water bath. Transfer to an ice cream base in a Pacojet beaker and freeze. Before serving, pacotize the ice cream. (Alternatively, prepare the ice cream in an ice cream maker according to the instructions or pour the ice cream base into a mold and put in the freezer. During the first few hours, stir vigorously several times. Just before serving, remove the ice cream from the freezer and let it thaw a little.)

Carrot cake
Preheat the oven to 350°F (180°C). Beat the egg and sugar until frothy. Mix the flour, almonds, and baking powder and stir into the egg and sugar mixture in batches, then mix in the oil, carrots, and ginger. Pour the dough into a rectangular cake pan lined with baking paper and bake for at least 40 minutes. Before serving, cut the cake into rectangles.

Carrot and vanilla puree
Peel and roughly chop the carrots. Slice open the vanilla bean lengthwise, scrape out the seeds and set them aside. Put the carrot pieces, 2 grams salt, sugar, and vanilla pod in a foil bag, vacuum seal and cook in a steam oven preheated to 212°F (100°C) for 70 minutes until soft. Take the carrots out of the vacuum bag and remove the vanilla pod. In a food processor or blender, finely puree the carrots, the vanilla seeds that were set aside, and the lemon juice. Season again with salt and sugar and bind with the xanthan gum. Pass the puree through a fine-mesh strainer and transfer to a piping bag.

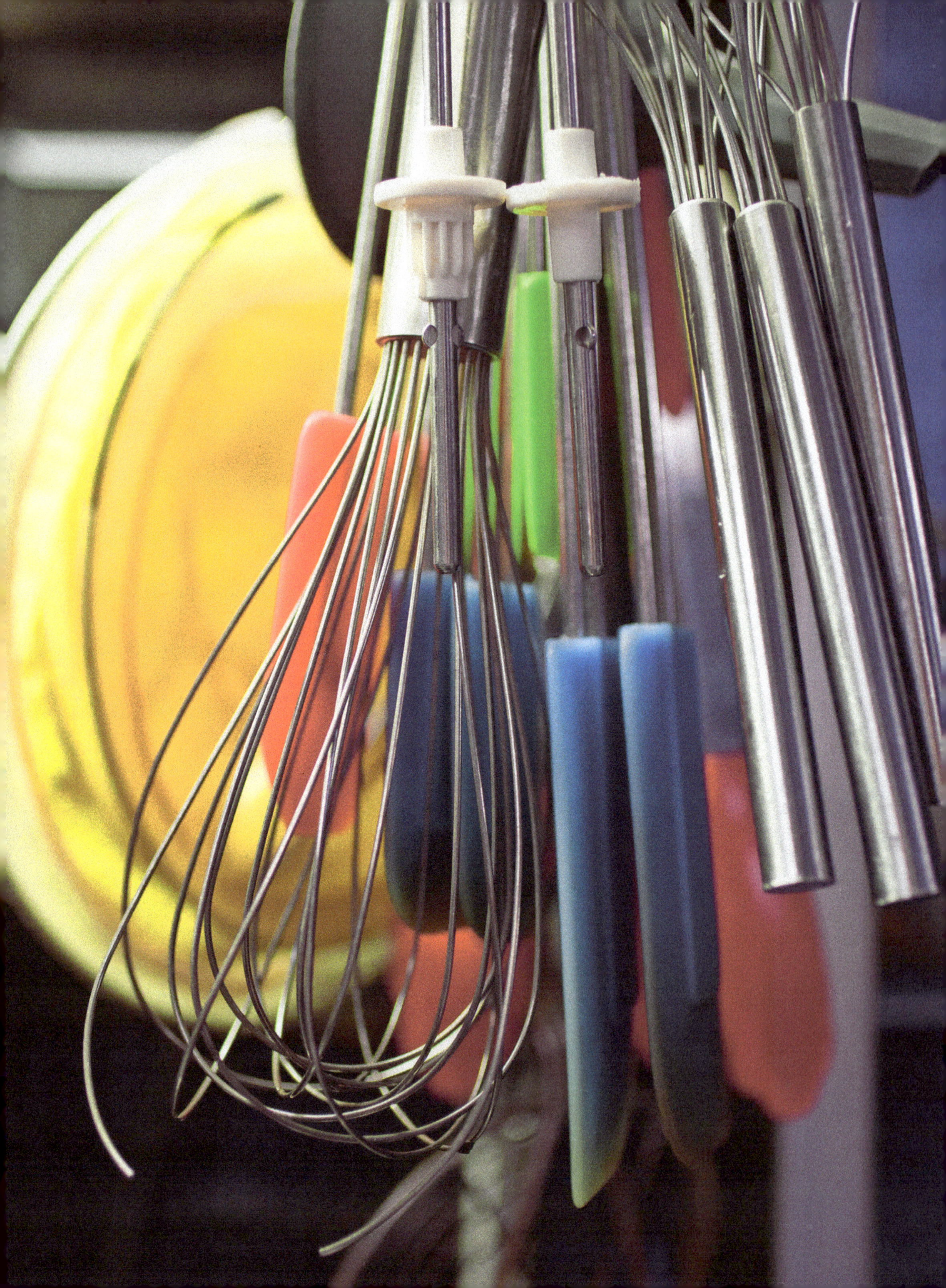

For the pandan crème
10 g pandan leaves
65 g white chocolate
  couverture
1 sheet white gelatin
75 g coconut milk
100 g cream
Juice from 1/2 lime
1 pinch of salt

For the pineapple chutney
1/4 pineapple, peeled and
  cored
15 g fresh peeled ginger
1/2 chili pepper, with the
  seeds removed
40 g sugar
20 g dry white wine
80 mL pineapple juice plus
  some more for thickening
1/4 teaspoon cornstarch
  Salt

For the ginger gel
300 g ginger puree
100 g lemon juice
130 g pineapple juice
35 g brown sugar
5.5 g agar flakes or powder
2 g gellan gum
1 pinch of salt

For the caramelized
  pineapple
1 pineapple
2 tablespoons brown sugar

To serve
Coconut and carrot crumble
Sorrel leaves

Pandan crème
Chop the pandan leaves and couverture into small pieces. Soften the gelatin in cold water. Bring the coconut milk to a boil and pour it over the pandan leaves and couverture while still hot. Stir until the couverture has dissolved. Stir the gelatin into the warm mixture. Add the cold cream, lime juice, and salt. Let the mixture cool, pass through a fine-mesh strainer and transfer to a piping bag. Chill until serving.

Pineapple chutney
Finely dice the pineapple, ginger, and chili pepper. In a saucepan, let the sugar caramelize, deglaze with the white wine and let it boil briefly until the caramel has dissolved. Then add the pineapple, ginger, and chili cubes. Pour in pineapple juice and simmer briefly. Thicken with a little cornstarch mixed in pineapple juice and season with a little salt.

Ginger gel
Bring all ingredients to a boil and set aside to cool. Place the gel in a food processor and puree. Before serving, transfer the puree into a piping bag.

Caramelized pineapple
Cut the pineapple into 6-mm thick slices and cut out circles with a serving ring (about 3 cm in diameter). Sprinkle the sugar on a flat bowl. Before serving, dip a cut surface of the pineapple in the sugar and caramelize the sugar layer with a kitchen torch.

To serve
Place a piece of carrot cake on each plate. Add a few dollops of carrot and vanilla puree and ginger gel as well as a dollop of pandan crème. Place some pineapple chutney on top of the cake and place a scoop of pandan ice cream on top. Garnish with the coconut and carrot crumble and sorrel leaves.

Five-Spice Panna Cotta

Serves 4 | Prep time: 2 ½ hours plus 1 day to freeze the sorbet

For the mandarin sorbet
350 g mandarin puree
70 g lime juice
120 g brown sugar
8 g Pectagel Rose
40 g glucose powder
1 pinch of salt

For the sesame seed cookie
60 g maple syrup
60 g butter
60 g oatmeal
40 g white sesame seeds
60 g cake flour
75 g sugar
25 g grated coconut
2 g salt
4 g green tea powder
2.5 g baking powder

For the five-spice panna cotta
2 sheets white gelatin
125 g white chocolate
  couverture
350 g cream
1 kaffir lime leaf
1 1/2 teaspoons five-spice
  powder
15 g lime juice
1 pinch of salt

For the chocolate crème
1 sheet white gelatin
150 g dark chocolate
  couverture (>60% cocoa
  solids)
90 g whole milk
60 g egg yolks
140 g crème fraîche

Mandarin sorbet
Bring all ingredients to a boil in 1 cup (250 mL) water. Transfer into a Pacojet beaker and freeze. Before serving, pacotize the ice cream. (Alternatively, prepare the sorbet in an ice cream maker according to the instructions or pour the sorbet base into a mold and put in the freezer. During the first few hours, stir vigorously several times. Just before serving, remove the sorbet from the freezer and let it thaw a little.)

Sesame seed cookie
Knead all ingredients with 2 teaspoons of hot water. Preheat the oven to 315°F (155°C). Roll the dough out flat onto a silicone baking mat and bake for 20 minutes. Let the cookies cool a bit and break them into small pieces. Dry overnight in a dehydrator.

Five-spice panna cotta
Soften the gelatin in cold water. Roughly chop the couverture. Stir the kaffir lime leaves into ½ cup (120 g) cream and bring to a boil. Pour over the couverture and let it dissolve completely while stirring. Squeeze out the gelatin and mix it into the hot chocolate crème mixture. Stir the rest of the cold cream 1 cup (230 grams) into the mixture, then add in the lime juice and salt.

Pour the panna cotta about 5-mm high into a mold (30 x 30 cm) and refrigerate. Cut circles out of the dough with a round cookie or biscuit cutter (8-cm in diameter).

Chocolate crème
Soften the gelatin in cold water. Chop the couverture and dissolve over a water bath. Emulsify some milk with the egg yolk over a water bath. Gradually add the gelatin, melted couverture,

>

50 g butter
25 g raw sugar
140 g Crème fraîche
50 g butter
25 g raw sugar
1 pinch of chili powder
1 pinch of salt

For the mandarin foam
1 1/2 sheets of white gelatin
50 g coconut milk
15 g brown sugar
100 g mandarin puree
25 g calamansi puree
  (calamondin orange)
75 g egg whites
1 pinch of salt

For the preserved
  mandarin oranges
100 mL mandarin puree
25 mL calamansi puree
  (calamondin orange)
15 mL lime juice
1 stalk lemongrass
25 g brown sugar
Seeds from 1 vanilla bean
1 pinch xanthan gum
12 mandarin orange sections

For the mandarin gel
175 g mandarin puree
15 g lime juice
25 g calamansi puree
  (calamondin orange)
1 stalk lemongrass
25 g brown sugar
2.3 g agar flakes or powder
1 g gellan gum

To serve
Red Oxalis

remaining milk, crème fraîche, butter, sugar, chili powder, and salt. Pour the chocolate crème into conical silicone molds and refrigerate.

Mandarin foam
Soften the gelatin in cold water. Bring the coconut milk and sugar to a boil and dissolve the squeezed-out gelatin in it. Mix the remaining ingredients into the coconut milk, then pass through a fine-mesh strainer, pour it into a siphon bottle and screw on 2 capsules. Chill for at least 2 hours before using.

Preserved mandarin oranges
In a saucepan, bring the fruit purees, lime juice, lemongrass, sugar, and seeds from the vanilla pod to a boil. Thicken with the xanthan gum, add the mandarin sections and bring to a boil, then set aside in the stock to cool.

Mandarin gel
Let all the ingredients simmer for 3 minutes. Set aside to cool. Then puree the gel in a food processor or blender until smooth. Before serving, transfer the puree into a piping bag.

To serve
Place 2 slices of five-spice panna cotta on the plate and crumble some sesame cookie pieces over them. Arrange a few dollops of the mandarin gel, two scoops of chocolate crème, and three preserved mandarin sections on the plate. Place a small scoop of mandarin sorbet and some mandarin foam on top. Garnish with the oxalis leaves.

"Yoso-Style" Banana

Serves 4 | Prep time: 2 ½ hours plus 1 day to freeze the parfait and to cool the ganache

For the banana parfait
25 g egg yolks
15 g egg whites
50 g sugar
175 mL cream
75 g banana puree
Juice from 1/2 lime
1 shot of white rum

For the banana ganache
150 g white chocolate
175 g cream
40 g coconut milk
50 mL banana pure

For the cinnamon bud foam
1 teaspoon cinnamon buds
10 black peppercorns
¼ cinnamon stick
12 g brown sugar
Salt
250 mL coconut milk
1 sheet white gelatin

For the banana gel
175 g banana juice
100 g banana puree
25 g lime juice
1 pinch turmeric
3 g agar flakes or powder
1.5 g gellan gum

For the batter
75 g cake flour
5 g sugar
75 mL whole milk
25 mL coconut milk
25 g whole egg
12 g egg whites
1 pinch of salt
Neutral vegetable oil for
  frying

Banana parfait
Mix the egg yolks, egg whites, and sugar over a water bath until frothy, then continue stirring over ice water until cold. Whip the cream until stiff. Mix the banana puree, lime juice, and rum into the egg mixture. Gradually fold in the whipped cream. Transfer the parfait into cylindrical silicone molds (60 x 40 mm) and freeze. Before serving, remove the parfait from the molds.

Banana ganache
Roughly chop the chocolate. Bring the cream, coconut milk, and banana puree to a boil. Pour over the chocolate and dissolve it completely while stirring. Mix with a hand blender and then chill for at least 4 hours. Before serving, beat until stiff with a hand mixer and transfer to a piping bag.

Cinnamon bud foam
Crush the cinnamon buds and peppercorns with a mortar and pestle. In a saucepan, add the coconut milk, cinnamon, brown sugar, a pinch of salt, and bring it to a boil, then let simmer gently for 3 minutes. Remove from the stove and let the coconut milk steep for 30 minutes. Soak the gelatin in cold water, squeeze out the water, and dissolve it in the still warm coconut milk. Pass the coconut milk through a fine-mesh strainer, pour it into a siphon bottle and screw on 2 capsules. Before serving, chill for at least 2 hours.

Banana gel
Bring all of the ingredients to a boil and let them cool. In a food processor or blender, mix into a smooth gel. Transfer to a piping bag.

Batter
Mix all of the ingredients into a homogeneous, slightly liquid dough. Heat the oil to 320°F (160°C) and drizzle in small portions of dough so that small strands are formed. Lift the golden brown strands out of the oil with a slotted spoon and drain on paper towels.

For the marinated banana
1 small ripe banana
2 tablespoons banana gel
  (see above)

To serve
Green oxalis

Marinated banana
Peel the bananas and cut it into very small cubes. Mix the banana cubes with the banana gel.

To serve
Place two banana parfait cylinders on the plate. Place a dollop of cinnamon bud foam next to a parfait cylinder, two dollops of banana ganache next to the others, and a few dollops of banana gel around the plate. Arrange the fried strands of dough on the parfait. Add 2 teaspoons of marinated banana and garnish with the oxalis leaves.

Hiramasa Sashimi | Asparagus | Mizuna

Serves 4 | Prep time: 1 ½ hours plus 1 day to pickle the vegetables

For the pink radish
30 g sugar
30 mL rice vinegar
1 pink radish

For the green asparagus
salad
12 green asparagus stalks
1 tablespoon neutral
   vegetable oil
50 g white sesame seeds
50 g sesame paste
30 mL soy sauce
30 mL rice vinegar
30 g sugar
Some mizuna lettuce
   (Japanese mustard greens)

For the white asparagus
salad
1 red chili pepper
30 mL sesame oil
4 g grated fresh ginger
70 mL rice vinegar
50 mL sugar
Salt
Freshly ground black
   pepper
4 white asparagus stalks

Pink radish
Dissolve the sugar in the vinegar while stirring. Using a mandolin or slicer, peel the radish and cut it lengthwise into very thin slices (<1 mm). Fill a foil bag with the radish slices and marinade, vacuum seal and marinate in the refrigerator for 1 day. Before serving, remove from the vacuum bag and drain. Cut the slices into 1.5-cm wide strips and trim the ends straight. Roll the strips up into tight spirals.

Green asparagus salad
Clean the asparagus. If necessary, peel the lower third and cut off the lower ends (about 1 cm). Heat the oil in a pan and sauté the asparagus in it for about 3 minutes. Shake occasionally so that the asparagus stalks get a little color on all sides. Remove from the pan to cool.

Toast the sesame seeds in a non-stick pan, without oil, allow to cool. Using a mortar and pestle, grind to a powder. Mix the sesame seeds with the sesame paste, soy sauce, rice vinegar, sugar, and ¼ cup (60 mL) water to create a marinade. Before serving, cut the cold asparagus stalks into 4-cm long pieces and marinate with the sesame dressing and the lettuce tips.

White asparagus salad
Clean and core the chili pepper and cut into thin rings. Mix the chili rings with the sesame oil, ginger, rice vinegar, and sugar, and season with salt and pepper. Peel the asparagus and cut off the lower ends (about 0.5 cm). Using a peeler, cut the asparagus stalks lengthwise into fine strips. Before serving, marinate the asparagus strips with the sesame oil dressing.

>

For the Hiramasa kingfish
  sashimi

2 tablespoons white sesame
  seeds
200 g hiramasa kingfish
  (yellowtail kingfish)
2 tablespoons toasted
  sesame oil
Maldon sea salt

To serve
Green oxalis

Hiramasa sashimi

Toast the sesame seeds in a non-stick pan, without oil, allow
to cool and grind to powder with a mortar and pestle. Cut the
hiramasa sashimi in 5-mm thin slices. Brush the fish slices with a
little sesame oil, salt them, and sprinkle sesame seeds over them.

To serve

Form a bed from the marinated mizuna salad and the green and
white asparagus. Arrange three slices of hiramasa sashimi on top
in the shape of a fan. Scatter a few of the pink radish spirals on
the plates and garnish with green oxalis leaves.

Bulgogi-style Mackerel | Romaine Lettuce | Pearl Onions

Serves 4 | **Prep time:** 2 ½ hours plus 1 day to pickle the vegetables

For the onion crunch
1 white onion
2 tablespoons tempura flour
Neutral vegetable oil for
  frying

For the sweet potato puree
500 g sweet potatoes
Salt
Some freshly squeezed
  lime juice
Ground chili peppers

For the pearl onions
50 mL rice vinegar
50 mL apple juice
50 g sugar
100 g pearl onions

Onion crunch
Peel the onion and cut into 2-mm slices. Dust the rings with the tempura flour. Heat the oil in a saucepan to 320°F (160°C) and cook the slices in batches until they are golden brown. Drain on paper towels, then let dry in a dehydrator. Store in an airtight container.

Sweet potato puree
Preheat the oven to 355°F (180°C). Bake the sweet potatoes in an ovenproof dish for about 1 1/2 hours until soft. Peel off the skins. Transfer into a food processor or blender, adding a little salt, lime juice, and chili powder, puree until reaches a very fine consistency. Pass the puree through a fine-mesh strainer, transfer to a piping bag and keep warm until serving.

Pearl onions
Mix the rice vinegar, apple juice, and sugar until the sugar has dissolved. Peel the pearl onions, bring them to a boil with the stock and simmer for 5 minutes. Let the pearl onions cool in the stock, transfer to a foil bag, vacuum seal and let sit for 1 day. Then remove the pearl onions from the vacuum bag, cut them in half and divide into individual portions. Before serving, briefly ignite the onions with a kitchen torch.

\>

For the mandarin gelée

50 mL mandarin orange
  juice
3 g vegetarian gelatin
  powder

For the Bulgogi-style
  mackerel

15 g sugar
40 mL mirin (rice wine)
2 g salt
4 mackerel filets (approx.
  150–200 grams)
10 g white sesame seeds
1 green onion
1 clove of garlic
180 mL soy sauce
10 g black peppercorns,
  crushed
30 mL toasted sesame oil
40 mL pear juice
1 teaspoon tapioca starch

Mandarin gelée

Bring the juice and gelatin to a boil and pour into a small, angular mold so that the liquid is about 6-mm high. Chill the gelée. Before serving, cut into 6 x 6-mm cubes.

Bulgogi-style mackerel

Mix the sugar, mirin, and salt well until everything has dissolved. Carefully examine the mackerel fillets for bones and remove them, then submerge the fillets in the mirin marinade. Allow the fish fillets to sit for 20 minutes. Under cold running water, carefully rinse off the marinade and pat the fish fillets dry.

For the bulgogi marinade, lightly toast the sesame seeds in a non-stick pan, without oil. Trim the green onions and cut the white part into thin rings. Peel and finely chop the garlic. Mix the sesame seeds, green onion, soy sauce, garlic, pepper, sesame oil, and pear juice. Set aside 4 tablespoons marinade for the romaine lettuce. Place the mackerel fillets in a shallow bowl and pour the remaining bulgogi marinade over them so that they are completely covered. After 30 minutes, remove the mackerel fillets and drain well. Place the fillets next to each other on a baking sheet and briefly sear them on both sides with a kitchen torch before serving. For the bulgogi sauce, in a saucepan, bring ½ cup (100 mL) bulgogi marinade to a boil and thicken with the tapioca starch and 1 tablespoon of cold water.

For the purple sweet potatoes

1 chili pepper
1/2 stalk lemongrass
100 mL passion fruit juice
100 mL apple juice
50 grams sugar
100 grams rice vinegar
10 mL soy sauce
1 purple sweet potato

For the romaine lettuce

2 hearts of romaine lettuce
1 tablespoon neutral
  vegetable oil
4 tablespoons bulgogi
  marinade (see above)

To serve

Pickled red onion (see
  "Fried Calamaretti |
  Lettuce | Celery, p. 240)

Purple sweet potatoes

Clean, dry, and remove the seeds from the chili pepper. Chop the pepper very finely. Rinse, trim the root end, and finely chop the lemongrass. Mix the passion fruit juice, apple juice, sugar, rice vinegar, soy sauce, chili pepper, and lemongrass until the sugar has dissolved. Peel the sweet potatoes and cut into 8-mm thick slices. Bring the marinade to boil and cook the sweet potato slices for 4 minutes until soft, then remove from the heat to cool. Before serving, cut the sweet potato slices into appealing shapes and cook them briefly on all sides in a non-stick pan, without oil.

Romaine lettuce

Trim, clean, and dry the lettuce. Cut the lettuce hearts in half. Heat the oil in a pan and sauté the lettuce, cut side down. Deglaze with bulgogi marinade.

To serve

Place the mackerel fillets on plates and arrange three dollops of sweet potato puree on each. Spread the pearl onions, the pickled red onions, and the purple sweet potatoes out evenly next to them. Put one half of the romaine lettuce and two mandarin gelée cubes on the plate. Drizzle a few dots of bulgogi sauce and garnish with a little onion crunch.

Beef Tartare | Egg | Sesame | Spinach

Serves 4 | Prep time: 1 ½ hours plus 1 day to pickle the vegetables

For the sweet and sour radishes

4 radishes
30 g sugar
30 mL rice vinegar

For the zucchini slices in Korean marinade

1 teaspoon white sesame seeds
3 cloves garlic
120 mL soy sauce
60 mL toasted sesame oil
60 g sugar
0 g chili-bean sauce
20 g gochujang (spicy Korean chili paste)
1 zucchini
2 tablespoons peanut oil

For the caramelized peanuts "demi-sel"

50 g peanuts
50 g powdered sugar
1 pinch of Maldon sea salt flakes

For the beef tartare

240 g beef tenderloin
Korean marinade (see above)
1 pinch of salt

Sweet and sour radishes

Clean, trim, dry, and cut the radishes into eighths. Dissolve the sugar in the rice vinegar while stirring. Pour the radishes and marinade into a foil bag, vacuum seal and marinate in the refrigerator for 1 day.

Zucchini slices in Korean marinade

For the Korean marinade, lightly toast the sesame seeds in a non-stick pan, without oil. Roughly chop the garlic. In a saucepan, mix the sesame seeds, garlic, soy sauce, sesame oil, sugar, chili bean sauce, and gochujang and bring to a boil. Remove from heat and let steep for 20 minutes. Pass through a fine-mesh strainer. Set aside about a third for the beef tenderloin. Clean and peel the zucchini and cut into 7-mm thick slices. In a saucepan, heat the peanut oil and sauté the zucchini slices on both sides over medium-high heat. Deglaze with the rest of the marinade, then immediately remove the zucchini and place next to each other on a baking sheet to cool.

Caramelized peanuts using Breton demi sel butter

Roughly chop the peanuts. Heat a stainless steel saucepan and roast the peanuts in it. Sprinkle powdered sugar over it, let the sugar caramelize, and season with the salt. Spread the caramelized peanuts on a sheet of parchment paper and let cool. Before serving, chop into desired size.

Beef tartare

Grind the beef with a knife by slicing it thinly against the grain, then cutting each slice into fine strips and then, finally, dicing those strips as finely as you can. Mix the tartare with the marinade and season to taste with a little salt.

>

For the spinach

80 g baby spinach
1/2 tablespoon neutral
  vegetable oil
1 teaspoon Korean marinade
  (see above)

For the poached egg yolks

4 eggs
Toasted sesame oil Maldon
  sea salt

To serve

Baby spinach leaves

Spinach

Clean, trim, and dry the spinach. In a pan, heat the oil, add the spinach to it to wilt. Season with the marinade

Poached egg yolks

Separate the eggs. Set the egg whites aside for use in another dish. Brush four small, heat-resistant ramekins with a little sesame oil and slide one egg yolk into each. Pour boiling water over the egg yolks in the ramekins and let stand for 3 minutes. Carefully remove the egg yolks with a spoon, season with 1 pinch of salt each and serve immediately on top of the spinach (see below).

To serve

Arrange the zucchini slices into a circle on each plate. Place the tartar on top with the help of a serving ring. Place the spinach on top of the tartare and place the poached egg yolks on top of the spinach. Garnish with the caramelized peanuts, radishes, and baby spinach.

TIP

The marinating time for pickled radishes can take longer than is specified; this will make the color more intense.

Soba Noodles | Red Shrimp | Calamaretti | Red Pepper Sauce

Serves 4 | **Prep time:** 2 hours plus 1 day to pickle the vegetables

For the pepper sauce
10 g white sesame seeds
1 clove of garlic
50 g gochujang (spicy Korean chili paste)
150 mL soy sauce
8 g red pepper flakes
15 g sugar
10 mL toasted sesame oil
15 g malt syrup

For the soba noodles
160 g soba noodles
1/4 head bok choy
2 tablespoons neutral vegetable oil

For the shrimp and calamaretti
Squid
8 raw shrimp
8 calamaretti tubes
2 tablespoons neutral vegetable oil
Salt
Freshly squeezed lime juice
Chili oil (if desired)

Red pepper sauce
Toast the sesame seeds in a non-stick pan, without oil. Peel and finely chop the garlic. Mix the sesame seeds and garlic together with the spice paste, soy sauce, red pepper flakes, sugar, sesame oil, and malt syrup.

Soba noodles
Cook the soba noodles in boiling water for 3 minutes, pass through a fine-mesh strainer and rinse with cold water, then drain well. Trim, clean, and dry the bok choy. Cut fine julienne strips from the bok choy. Heat the oil in a pan and add the bok choy, soba noodles, and 3 tablespoons of red pepper sauce (see above) and stir well.

Shrimps and calamaretti
Clean, devein, and peel the shrimp. In a large saucepan, heat 1 tablespoon of olive oil. Briefly sauté the shrimp. Season to taste with a little salt and fresh lime juice. If desired, season with a little chili oil for more heat. Clean the calamaretti. Remove the outer skin and viscera from the tubes, briefly rinse under cold running water. Remove the eyes, beak, and backbone (if it has one). Cut the tube lengthwise and carefully score the inside in a crosshatch pattern without cutting all the way through. Heat the remaining olive oil (1 tablespoon) in another pan. Briefly sear the tubes and tentacles. Season to taste with a little salt and fresh lime juice. Season with chili oil for more heat.

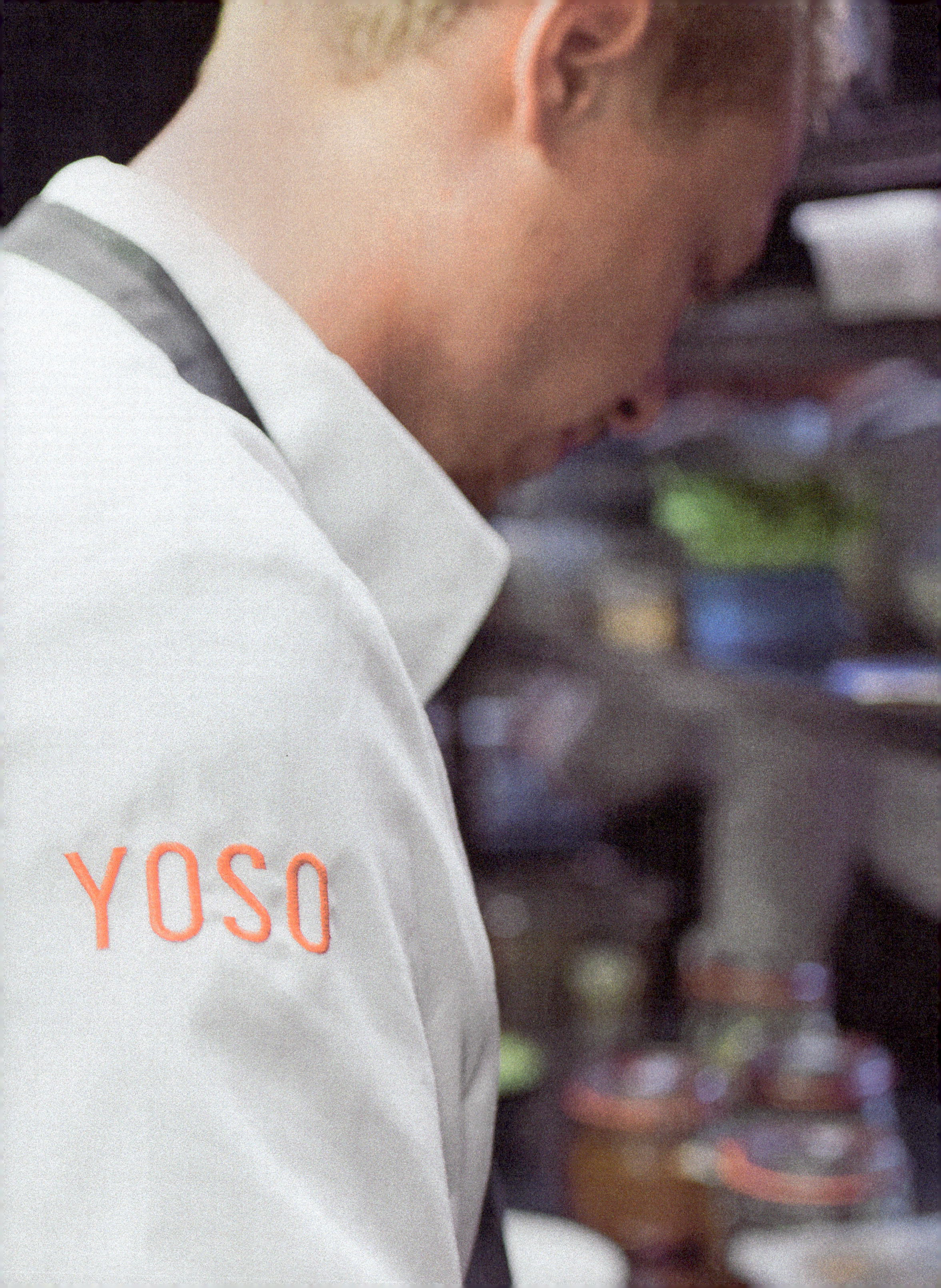
YOSO

Pink radish (see "Hiramasa
  Sashimi| Asparagus|
  Mizuna" on p. 280)
Nasturtium
Green part of spring onions,
  cut into rings

To serve
Use a fork to twist the soba noodles into shapely strands and place
one strand on each plate. Scatter the calamaretti and shrimp on
top. Shape the radish slices like flowers and insert them in between.
Garnish with nasturtiums and rings from the green part of the
green onion.

TIPS

The dish can also be served as a main
course. Simply increase the number of
shrimp and calamaretti to 12 each and
the soba noodles to 280 grams.

Be careful when moving the soba noodles
in the pan with tongs or spoon, because
the noodles break easily and then can
no longer be twisted decoratively on the
plate.

Pork Belly BBQ | Perilla Leaves | Radish

Serves 4 | Prep time: 2 hours plus 1 day to marinate the meat
plus 36 hours for sous-vide cooking

For the pork belly
3 green onions
4 cloves garlic
5 black peppercorns
4 red chili peppers
120 mL light soy sauce
60 g brown sugar
30 g liquid honey
10 g salt
120 mL toasted sesame oil
700 mL pear juice
1.5 kg pork belly with rind

For the radish kimchi
100 g sugar
50 mL fish sauce
50 mL corn oil
1 tablespoon sambal oelek
1 teaspoon gochugaru
  (Korean chili flakes)
1 tablespoon gochujang
  (spicy Korean chili paste)
1 teaspoon Togarashi spice
  mixture
50 mL chili sauce
1 daikon radish

Pork belly
Rinse, trim the root end, and finely chop the green onions. Mince the garlic cloves, grind the peppercorns coarsely, clean the chili peppers and cut into small pieces with the seeds. In a bowl, mix the green onions, garlic, pepper, chili peppers, soy sauce, sugar, honey, salt, sesame oil and pear juice together well. Put the pork belly and marinade in a foil bag, vacuum seal and marinate in the refrigerator for 24 hours. Preheat a water bath to 150°F (64°C). Cook the vacuum-packed pork belly in the water bath for 36 hours. Remove the pork belly from the bag and drain well. Discard the liquid. Place the meat flat on a plate to cool and weigh it down with another plate. Before serving, cut the pork belly into thin strips. You will need about 240 grams of the pork belly. The remaining pork belly can be saved for
use in another dish. Stir fry the strips on all sides in a hot pan. Add some ssamjang paste (see below) into the pan and toss everything until well coated.

Radish kimchi
In a saucepan, mix the sugar and fish sauce, stirring until the sugar has dissolved. Add the oil and spices, bring to a boil. Remove from heat. Let cool. Using a mandolin or slicer, peel the radish and cut it lengthwise into very thin slices (<1 mm). Pour the radish slices and half of the marinade into a foil bag, vacuum seal and marinate for 1 day.

>

BBQ
2lc

Malcolm

For the ssamjang paste

1 heaping teaspoon of white
  sesame seeds
3 cloves garlic
40 g fresh ginger
40 g soybean paste
40 g gochujang (spicy
  Korean chili paste)
40 g toasted sesame oil
40 g malt syrup
35 mL apple juice

To serve

To serve Pink radish
  (see "Hiramasa Sashimi |
  Asparagus | Mizuna" on
  p. 284)
Perilla leaves

Ssamjang paste

Toast the sesame seeds in a non-stick pan, without oil. Peel and mince the garlic cloves. Peel and finely chop the ginger. Mix the sesame seeds, garlic, ginger, soybean paste, gochujang, sesame oil, malt syrup, and apple juice.

To serve

To garnish, overlap three perilla leaves on each of the plates. Place three strips of radish kimchi, pork belly, and pink radish on top of each other.

TIP

Korean BBQ is so popular in Korea that it made me really want to serve it back home in Germany. The idea behind the perilla leaves is that you can wrap the pork belly in it and eat it directly with your hands.

Duck | Korean Banchan

Serves 4 | Prep time: 2 hours plus 1 day to pickle the vegetables

For the cucumber kimchi
1/2 cucumber
2 pinches of salt
2 tablespoons kimchi
   marinade (see "Marinated
   and Slow Cooked Pork
   Belly |Kimchi with Apple
   on p. 304)

For the duck breast
2 duck breasts (180 g each)
2 tablespoons neutral
   vegetable oil Maldon sea
   salt

For the lotus root
1 lotus root (approx. 200g)
100 mL apple juice
100 mL passion fruit juice
1/4 teaspoon vitamin C
   powder
2 kaffir lime leaves
2 tablespoons neutral
   vegetable oil

Cucumber kimchi
Quarter the cucumber lengthwise and remove the seeds. Cut the cucumber lengthwise again into thirds and then cut the sticks into cubes. Mix the cucumber cubes with the salt and let it sit for 30 minutes. Pass the cucumbers through a fine-mesh strainer and then put the cubes and the kimchi marinade in a foil bag, vacuum seal and leave to marinate for 1 day.

Duck breast
Preheat oven to 250°F (120°C). Place the duck breasts with the meat side down on a tray and bake them in the oven for 12-16 minutes, depending on the size, while checking the core temperature (125°F / 52°C). Then let the duck breasts rest for 15 minutes in a hold-o-mat. (Alternatively, keep them warm in an oven that is approx. 170°F / 75°C.) Before serving, heat the oil in a pan and cook the duck breasts, skin side down, for 2–3 minutes or until crispy. Then turn the breasts and cook them briefly on the meat side. Carve and season with salt.

Lotus root
Peel the lotus root and cut into rounds. Check the "air holes" and clean if necessary. Bring the fruit juices, vitamin C powder, and lime leaf to a boil, and cook the lotus root slices for 20 minutes or until al dente. Remove the lotus root rounds from the liquid and drain well. Heat the oil in a pan and stir fry the lotus root in it.

For the zucchini with sesame

1 zucchini
2 tablespoons toasted
  sesame oil
Salt
Sugar
Rice vinegar
2 tablespoons white sesame
  seeds

For the tofu with spicy sauce

45 g sugar
90 mL soy sauce
90 g gochujang (spicy
  Korean chili paste)
60 mL pear juice
1 pinch xanthan gum
200 g silken tofu
Tempura flour
4 tablespoons neutral
  vegetable oil

To serve

Green onion, green part
  only, cut into thin rings

Zucchini with sesame

Cut the zucchini into 4-mm thin slices. Heat the sesame oil in a pan and stir fry the zucchini in it until translucent. Season the zucchini with salt, sugar, and a little rice vinegar. Toast the sesame seeds in a pan, without oil. Before serving, pour the sesame seeds over the zucchini slices and mix together.

Tofu with spicy sauce

Dissolve the sugar in the soy sauce, bring to a boil with the gochujang and pear juice and thicken with a little xanthan gum. Cut the tofu into eight blocks (about 2 x 4 x 1 cm each). In a bowl, toss the blocks in the tempura flour until coated on all sides. Heat the oil in a pan and cook the breaded tofu on all sides until golden brown.

To serve

Preheat four plates. Arrange two slices of duck breast and two blocks of tofu on each of the plates. Drizzle the hot sauce over the tofu and garnish with the green rings from the green onion. Place the zucchini with sesame seeds, the lotus root, and the cucumber kimchi in separate bowls.

Marinated and Braised Pork Belly | Kimchi with Apple

Serves 4 | Prep time: 2 hours plus 1 day to marinate the meat plus 36 hours for sous-vide cooking

For the pork belly

3 green onions
4 cloves garlic
4 red chili peppers 1
20 mL light soy sauce
60 g brown sugar
30 g liquid honey
10 grams salt
5 black peppercorns,
  coarsely ground
120 mL toasted sesame oil
700 mL pear juice
1.5 kg pork belly with rind

For the Napa cabbage kimchi

1 kg Napa cabbage
100 g salt
100 g sugar
50 mL fish sauce
50 mL corn oil
1 tablespoon sambal oelek
1 teaspoon gochugaru
  (Korean chili flakes)
1 tablespoon gochujang
  (spicy Korean chili paste)
1 teaspoon togarashi spice
  mix
50 mL chili sauce

Pork belly

Rinse, trim the root end, and finely chop the green onions. Peel and finely chop the garlic. Clean and dry the chili peppers and cut into small pieces with the seeds. Mix the green onions, garlic, chili peppers, soy sauce, sugars, honey, salt, pepper, sesame oil and pear juice in a bowl and stir until everything has dissolved. Cut the pork belly in half. Put each piece of meat and half of the marinade in a foil bag, vacuum seal and marinate in the refrigerator for 24 hours. Preheat the water bath to 150°F (64°C) and cook the vacuum-sealed pork belly in it for 36 hours. Then remove the meat from the two vacuum bags, and drain the stock. Lay the pork belly flat on a plate and weigh it down with a plate to cool.

Napa cabbage kimchi

Trim, quarter, and rinse the Napa cabbage. Cut out the stalk. In a large bowl, dissolve the salt in 800 mL of water. Dip the Chinese cabbage quarters in the water, carefully remove and place on a tray. Let the quarters marinade for 3 hours and turn four to five times in between. Then drain the Chinese cabbage through a sieve, rinse twice under running cold water and drain well. For the kimchi marinade, mix the sugar and fish sauce in a saucepan until the sugar has dissolved. Add the oil and spices, mix and bring to a boil. Let the marinade cool. Put the Napa cabbage quarters and the marinade (100 grams) in a foil bag, vacuum seal and marinate for at least 1 day.

\>

For the pork belly paste

2 cloves garlic (40 g)

20 g fresh ginger

20 g white sesame seeds

120 g gochugaru (Korean chili pepper flakes)

80 g gochujang (spicy Korean chili paste)

40 g soy sauce

40 g oyster sauce

40 g mirin (Japanese rice wine)

50 g sugar

10 g black peppercorns, crushed

40 g toasted sesame oil

100 mL apple juice

400 g slow cooked pork belly (see above)

To serve

Apples, finely sliced

Radishes, finely sliced

Pork belly paste

Mince the garlic. Peel and finely chop the ginger. Briefly toast the sesame seeds in a nonstick pan without oil, then let cool. Mix the garlic, ginger, and sesame seeds together with the spices and apple juice in a bowl until everything has dissolved, and a homogeneous paste has formed. Cut the pork belly into same-sized cubes (1.5 x 1.5 cm) and stir fry them on all sides in a hot pan, then add 1 teaspoon of pork belly paste and toss well.

To serve

Arrange the kimchi in a deep plate and place a few cubes of pork belly on top. Garnish with rolled-up apple and radish slices.

TIPS

The kimchi can be prepared in large quantities and kept on hand for use in different meals.

Simply fill an airtight jar with the rest of the kimchi marinade and store in a cool place. It can also be prepared using vegetables other than cabbage, such as cucumber or radish. The rest of the pork belly can be packed in an airtight container and stored in a cool place for at least 2 weeks. It can also be frozen.

AUTHENTIC KOREAN:
WHAT MY TRIP TAUGHT ME ABOUT KOREAN FOOD

Fermentation – the heart of Korean cuisine

Many foods are fermented in Korea. This is done for both the taste and, above all, the shelf life of these foods and therefore their availability even outside of their actual season. Many families enjoy preparing fermented or pickled dishes and pastes together, almost as if it were a party. What I like best about it is that I can make it with vegetables that are mostly harvested from my own garden. It reminds me of my childhood in the countryside, even if I didn't really appreciate it back then. I'm lucky, though, since even in Korea, many people don't have access to their own vegetable garden. That's because they lack either the space to grow food or the time to look after it. In doing so, you learn to appreciate a product that you have grown and harvested yourself much more than when you get it from the nearest supermarket shelf or local market.

"Son-mat"— "hand taste"

Korean food is often prepared by hand. This is supposed to impart a special flavor to the food, meaning that when you eat it you can tell if a dish has been prepared with heart. If you watch Jeong Kwan prepare food, you can very clearly observe what it means to prepare food with your heart. She "massages" the plants, some of which require only a bit of additional seasoning. I was able to experience and enjoy for myself just how flavorful dishes made in Jeong Kwan's kitchen are, which surely has something to do with the feelings and heart that the chef poured into making them.

Health

Koreans believe that many products work like medicine. Wild plants from the mountains, ginseng and dried herbs help them either get or stay healthy. Even my guide Jain repeatedly drew my attention to products that are good for stomach pain or other ailments.

Right temperature

I noticed that many dishes are still boiling or simmering when they're brought to finish cooking on a gas stove at the table. Jain explains that the right temperature is the key to the perfect taste. Since many side dishes or individual dishes are also served cold, this is a kind of "yin and yang" approach to eating.

Season

Korean dishes are always based on seasonal products. Koreans believe that only seasonal fruits and vegetables are of the best quality and therefore also the best taste. They completely tailor their menus to this, in all restaurant categories, from small street food stands to Michelin-starred restaurants. In addition, there are naturally pickled and fermented vegetables, and above all the wide varieties of kimchi. And kimchi is also made according to which vegetables are in season. The temple kitchen, in particular, relies on using only the products that the earth gives them and that they have collected themselves. They have to be fresh or prepared during the seasons when nature offers only a small selection of products.

Spicy – aromatic and spicy

The most important flavoring agents for the typical Korean heat are garlic, green peppers, red pepper flakes, red pepper powder, soy sauce, sesame seeds, toasted sesame oil, black pepper, rice vinegar, and ginger. The proportions of the different spices to each other and mixing one with another then create the special taste, which differs from region to region and from cook to cook and makes each dish unique.

Chopsticks

Once again, I learned something new. Almost all the chopsticks in Korea are flat and made of metal. They are made of metal, because many of the fermented foods would corode and discolor wooden sticks. I learned that the shape (whether flat or round) is a question of cost: Flat chopsticks are less expensive.

Soup

To my delight, soup is always served in Korea: morning, noon, and night. Often you can get a special soup made from fermented soybean paste (doenjang-jjigae) that is served with seaweed and tofu. It helps neutralize the sometimes spicy dishes. In addition, hot soup is good for the body. And: Something liquid should be served with every meal so that the individual ingredients can combine better. Another kind of "yin and yang" of eating.

Sharing and mixing

Sharing is an important part of Korean food culture. Each person gets their own bowl of rice, and all the other bowls and food are shared. This conveys a sense of togetherness without any conscious effort. It also imparts a feeling of home and family as well, because you have to look after and pay attention to each other. Many Korean dishes only reveal their perfection when the different ingredients are mixed together correctly. This holds true for the famous bibimbap too; it only tastes the way it should when everything is mixed together well.   **>**

This thought also guides me in my cooking. As a chef, I try to incorporate it into the structure of my dishes. I consider what individual components I need to put on the plate in order to give the guests exactly the taste I had in mind, without anyone having to explain it at the table for a long time. How a dish is served is intended to improve its appearance. But more than that, it's meant to help the guest get the most perfect taste possible on their fork or chopstick. You might say that I have "mixed" everything in advance, in the way that best delivers the perfect taste experience directly to the guest. If the guests then suddenly mixed it all over again at the table, I'd be pretty surprised. But in Germany, that's not likely to happen, since people don't expect to mix their own ingredients; basically, I relieve the guest of this work beforehand.

Clearly, creating new dishes is no easy task. If nothing else, let this thought guide you: simple dishes often taste best because they combine all textures and tastes on one spoon. The dishes that can only be enjoyed with a spoon are often the most delicious. I think immediately of our dish "beef tartare | egg | sesame | spinach." The aromatic and spicy tartare in combination with the creamy egg yolk, the umami of the miso foam, the sweet and sour pickled radishes, and the crispy texture of the caramelized peanut make this dish one of Yoso's "signature dishes." It's simply delicious.

INDEX

PYEONGCHANG

SEOUL

ANDONG

GYEONGJU

JEONJU

DAMYANG
BAMBOO

BUSAN

JINHAE

JEJU

INCHEON

SEOUL

ANDONG

ANDONG

BUSAN

BUSAN

You can find more information about your trip to Korea here:
Korea Tourism Organization – http://german.visitkorea.or.kr/
oder instagram@koreatourismus

ACKNOWLEDGMENTS

I learned a lot on this trip. And I learned a lot about myself. I'm home again and can look back on my journey, which was also a journey into myself. I'm much more aware of many things and am even more grateful for who I am and with whom I can share my life.

My biggest thanks go to my parents, the two people who paved the way for me in the first place. I thank them for supporting me at all times and in every situation. Your love and everything you have taught me have made me the person I am today. You are and will always be my home.

Special thanks also go to Petra & Rolf, who trusted me to do exactly the right thing to help Yoso continue to flourish. By giving me the platform and the freedom to develop myself creatively, I'm able to help make so many guests happy.

Thanks to my wonderful team at Yoso. You are like a family who support me and have my back, making it possible for me to go on such a trip at all. It means a lot to me to work with you and to master the small and big challenges together every day. Thanks to you, at the end of the day, I can say: I am happy to work with you.

I would also like to thank my editor, Sonya Mayer, and Christian Verlag. We have known each other for a number of years and have always stayed in contact with the thought that we may one day work on a book together. Sonya has always believed in me and this great project and has stuck with it. It's just as I had always envisoned.

I thank Jain Song from South Korea, my guide, who made my trip to Korea unique with her warmth and personality. Her support gave me unforgettable insight into Korean cuisine. But, above all, I thank her for the priceless emotional moments in which she stood by me. Our time together was short, but so intense that she has become like a little Korean sister to me.

I would like to thank Jan C. Brettschneider for the wonderful pictures, for capturing the experience, the countless impressions that I had, and his excellent photographic eye. And I also thank Jan for his patience with me, because it was certainly not easy to accompany me on my emotionally complicated trip to Korea.

I would like to thank Jeong Kwan Seunim. My encounter with you was so special and unforgettable. You showed me a new perspective on life and touched me so much that I never want to forget these moments with you. You radiated so much love for people and such warmth.

I would like to thank my husband Christian, who always had positive words for me from afar and who brings so much happiness to my life. Without him I would certainly some- times lose the courage to keep going, to be strong, and to do my best every day. Christian, you give me the support and the calm that I need to be the person that I am.

I would also like to say thank you to my guests. If our team at Yoso has managed to give you a great culinary experience and I can see your happy faces every day, then that is my greatest motivation. And I hope that through the stories that I have shared here that you got to know my place of birth a little better.

I highly recommend that anyone who gets the chance, should visit this land of many wonders and its wonderful people.

I look forward to seeing you at Yoso in Andernach, Germany – "somewhere between Cologne and Frankfurt

Yours truly,

CREDITS

Special thanks go to the publisher for supporting this book project:

Rani Cheema, "Cheema's Travel" –
www.cheemastravel.com

Jain Song
www.instagram.com/dynamicjainsong

O'ngo Food – www.ongofood.com

Anke Camps, the sales representative for ASA Porzellan, which made the wonderful plates for the food photoshoot in "Yoso."

We would also like to thank Zunsa Demgenski for writing the recipe titles in Korean script.

All pictures on the cover and the inside were taken by Jan C. Brettschneider, with the exception of: pages 7, 8 (both), 147, 195, 199, 201 – these photos were taken by Sarah Henke.
Page 205: Torsten Zimmermann
Map, pages 316–317: Shutterstock/Bluehousestudio
Paper background, cover, chapter openers and tips: shutterstock/Claudio Divizia

Product management: Sonya Mayer
Cover design, layout and typesetting:
   Helen Garner, Art & Weise, Munich, Germany
Recipe editing: Dr. Regina Rosskopf
Proofreading: Franziska Sorgenfrei
Reproduction: LUDWIG:media, Zell am See, Austria
Production: Barbara Uhlig
Photography: Jan C. Brettschneider
Collaboration with travelogues: Stephanie Bräuer
Partner management: Thomas Nehm

Did you enjoy this book? Please recommend it!

★ ★ ★ ★ ★

Tell your friends about it, tell your bookseller, and review it online. And if you have criticism, corrections, updates, we look forward to hearing from you at:

CLEVO Books,
530 Euclid Ave #45
Cleveland, Oh 44115
www.clevobooks.com

The German National Library has listed this publication in the German National Bibliography; detailed bibliographic data are available on the Internet at http://dnb.d-nb.de.

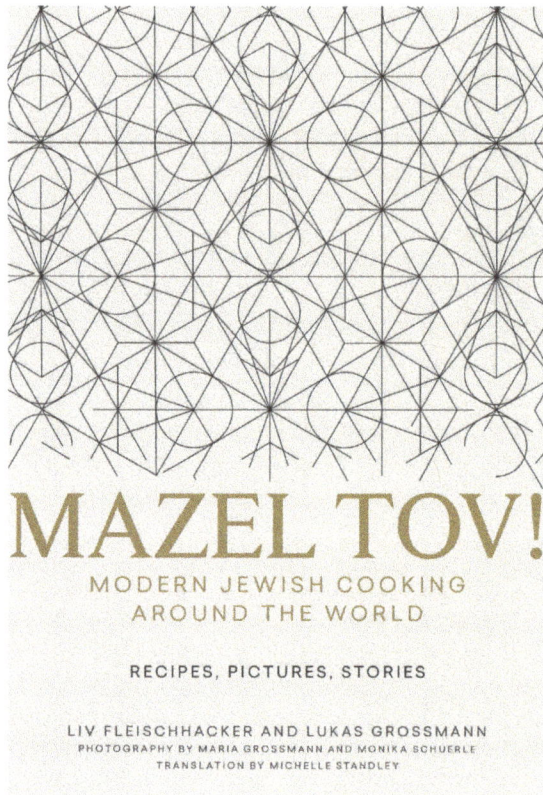

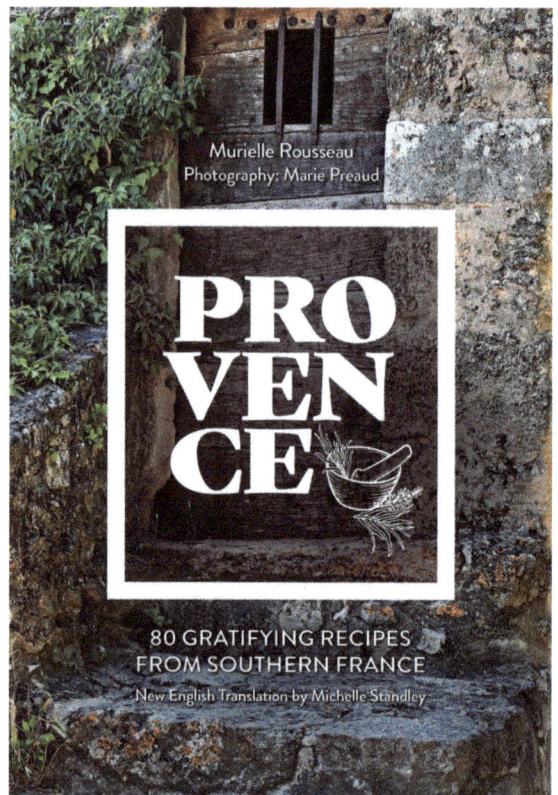

OTHER TITLES YOU MAY ENJOY
from

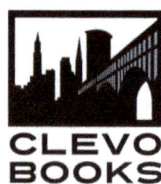

CULINA

an imprint of

CLEVO BOOKS

www.ingramcontent.com/pod-product-compliance
Lightning Source LLC
Chambersburg PA
CBHW040315100426
42811CB00012B/1453